The Niagara Gorge Belt I
A PICTORIAL ALBUM

Published by

Niagara Frontier Chapter, National Railway Historical Society

Edited by Gordon J. Thompson
2000

Dedicated to

Albert D. Kerr

Harold J. Ahlstrom

Laurence E. Burke

Gordon J. Thompson

Geoffrey W. Gerstung

The following have contributed photographs and information for this publication, for which the Chapter is deeply indebted:

Nelson Bauer collection
Buffalo & Erie County Historical Society
George Hamilton Forman
Richard Gillis
Sheldon S. King
Robert G. Lewis
John McCormick collection
Niagara Mohawk Power Corporation Archives
Richard A. Olday
David A. Scott
Edward Tanski
Ward Wood
William R. Gordon in his book   " 90 Years of Buffalo Railways"

Dale Bregger
Laurence E. Burke collection
Geoffrey W. Gerstung
Joseph Kellas
F.H. Leslie collection
John A. MacLean
John Mills
The Niagara Parks Commission (Ontario)
William L. Reddy
Russell H. Shapley collection
Gordon J.Thompson
Craig A. Woodworth

<u>Front Cover</u> In a Canadian open car as it moves south along the U.S. side of the turbulent Niagara River on its way from Lewiston to Niagara Falls. This car is about to stop in the Whirlpool Rapids Gorge to allow passengers to venture to the waters edge for a close-up of the frenzied thundering water.

<u>Back Cover</u> Tickets from the electric railways that served the Niagara Falls and Niagara Gorge area.

ISBN Number 0-9703552-0-3

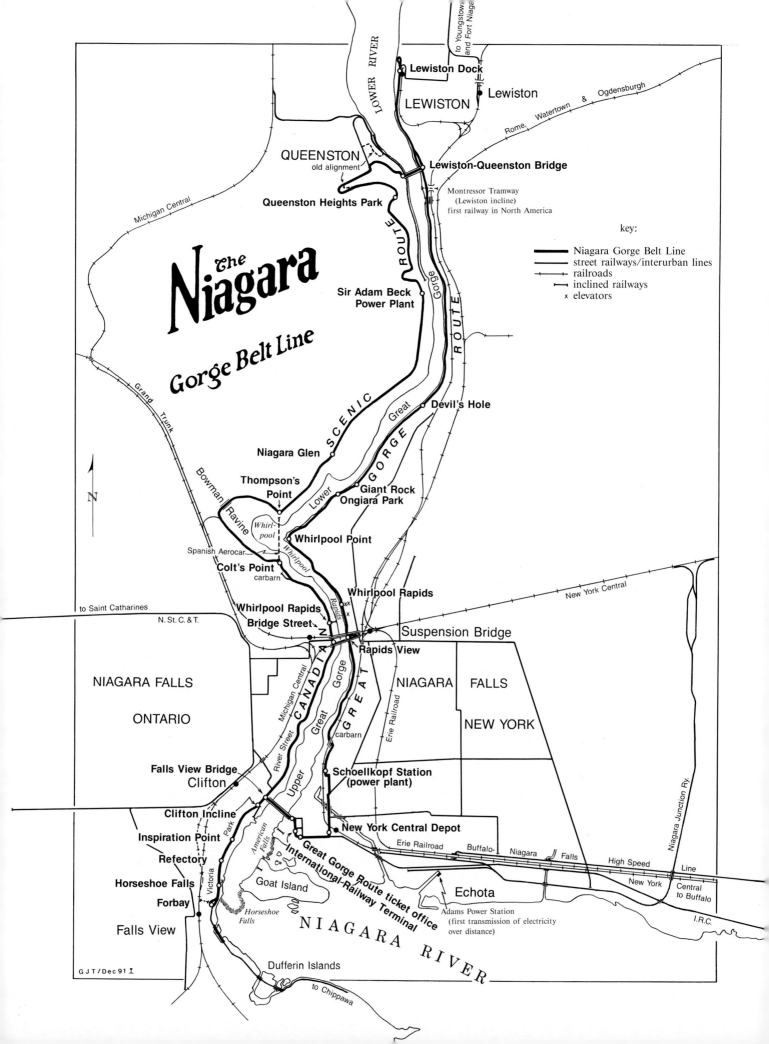

End of an Era: This rock slide, looking south from just north of the Grand Trunk (near) and Michigan Central (behind) railroad bridges, precipitated abandonment of the entire Niagara Gorge Railroad, last leg of the Niagara Gorge Belt Line, on September 17, 1935, after 40 years of service. In better years, the railroad company would have removed the obstruction.

THE NIAGARA GORGE BELT LINE

Introduction:

This book does not present a definitive history. It is an album of illustrations to help those who rode the popular trolleys through the magnificent Niagara Gorge remember the experience, and to show those who did not have the opportunity to ride this spectacular line what they missed.

A rock slide on a day late in the 1935 summer tourist season blocked the tracks of the Great Gorge Route section of the popular Niagara Gorge Belt Line trolley trip, bringing to a close 40 years of people access to one of the land's grandest bits of scenery. In the interim 65 years, these views have been available to only agile, hardy hikers. This book is devoted to those forty years when the general public, young and old, robust and frail, healthy and feeble enjoyed the most breath-taking, awe-inspiring journey possible in the world through sights, sounds, and experiences in intimate proximity to nature.

On August 31, 1932, the second of two twenty-year leases of the parkland through which the trolleys ran on the Canadian side of the Niagara River ended. At the height of the Depression, the International Railway Company had lost faith in the electric trolley car and was unwilling to invest in the relocation of its tracks as the Niagara Parks Commission would require in a renewal of the lease. The I.R.C. agreed, though, to operate the trolleys until September 11, 1932, so as not to disappoint expectant summer tourists. So ended the international

HISTORY

"Niagara Gorge Belt Line" service, although the Parks Commission did not remove the tracks until 1935. The cars continued on the American, "Great Gorge Route", side of the River. But the Niagara Falls Power Company, disenchanted owner of the Niagara Gorge Railroad Company, used the September 17, 1935, rock slide as a reason to bring down the final curtain on Gorge trolleys.

Why was the Niagara Gorge Belt Line built? The 35-mile Niagara River drops 326 feet throughout its course from Lake Erie between Fort Erie and Buffalo to Lake Ontario between Niagara-on-the-Lake and Fort Niagara. Nine miles of this course are rapids and waterfalls. At Niagara Falls, the water drops 167 feet over the Canadian -- or Horseshoe -- Falls and 193 feet over the American Falls. The force that carved the Niagara Gorge and the retreating Niagara Falls can be appreciated by considering that a major river emptying all the Great Lakes except Lake Ontario ranges up to 8,500 feet wide until it reaches the cataract. After its plunge, the volume of flow -- 250,000 cubic feet of water per second -- must then surge through a constricted canyon as narrow as 250 feet (at Niagara Glen). In effect, the river turns sideways and speeds up to let the water reach Lake Ontario.

This spectacle of nature has attracted people over a long period of time. They walked, rode horses, were carried in wagons and stage coaches, and came at least part way by lake boats and canal boats. This short stretch of border between two young nations became a focal point for railroads, providing a way for great numbers of people to more quickly and more conveniently reach the Falls. The advent of the electric trolley car, however, provided frequency and capacity previously unheard of. The Falls were quite easy to view. The railroad bridges provided teasing glimpses of the rapids below the Falls. Local entrepreneurs built primitive inclined railways and elevators -- usually water-powered -- to enable visitors to get to the water's edge at various points and be astounded by the tumultuous roaring Whirlpool Rapids.

The coming of the trolley was not limited to bringing curious people to this territory. The trolley builders went on to assure that everyone could gain a close-up impression of both the Falls and the Gorge. Soon travelers were being admonished, "One who simply views the Falls sees only a part of the wonders and beauties of Niagara, and "If you didn't see the Gorge, you didn't see Niagara."

Michigan Central Railroad passengers caught a glimpse of the Horseshoe Falls from the coach windows. Rome, Watertown & Ogdensburgh Railroad passengers were treated to a short ride high on the Gorge wall as their train descended to Lewiston. When the railroads promoted the passenger potential of these sights, the trolley entrepreneurs added that they had "The only railroad in the Canyon". When the automobile joined the means by which tourists reached the Niagara Frontier, they added, "There is no automobile road through the Gorge."

These admonitions are still true today, except that what the trolleys covered in two hours requires two days of strenuous hiking, much of it through extremely hazardous conditions.

The Niagara Gorge Belt Line operated a continuous tour over the tracks of several affiliated street railway companies. First to operate was the Niagara Falls Park & River Railway on the Canadian side of the Niagara River. In quick succession came the Niagara Gorge Railroad on the American side and the International Traction Company (later, International Railway Company -- I.R.C.) which built two bridges to complete the loop or "Belt". An affiliated venture was the Lewiston & Youngstown Frontier Railway. All became parts of the far-flung I.R.C. network.

Niagara Falls Park & River Railway Company/I.R.C. Park & River Division:

Financed by Canadian railroad interests and opened on May 24, 1893, the Niagara Falls Park & River Railway operated from Chippewa, passing the Falls and following the rim of the Gorge, to the Queenston steamship docks below the Niagara Escarpment. The company had rights to build south to Fort Erie across the river from Buffalo, and in 1894, extended the line up-river from Chippewa to Slater's Dock to meet steamships from Buffalo; this extension was removed about 1905, never having reached Fort Erie. The company did not exercise its rights to build a line through the Gorge at water level.

Nearly the entire line was through publicly-owned parkland for which privilege the railway paid an annual rent of $10,000 to the Queen Victoria Niagara Falls Park Commission

(Niagara Parks Commission after 1927). The 13-mile line was shortened to 11.4 miles by pulling back from Slater's Dock to a Michigan Central connection at Chippewa, and the initially single-track line was doubled wherever space allowed. Track was built to Canadian Pacific Railway standards. Electric power was generated at the company's own hydro-electric plant at the Falls. A seldom-used steam "booster" generating plant at Queenston assisted cars going up the steep escarpment when ship-loads of as many as 2,000 passengers had to be quickly taken south to the Falls.

At first, the line operated only during the warm seasons, but beginning in 1895, the company provided winter service, too.

The original cars of this railway were specially-built sightseeing trolleys. Their longitudinal seats, arranged in two rows, one higher than the other, faced one side of the car. These rolling bleachers were destroyed in a 1906 carbarn fire, and more conventional rolling stock was employed thereafter -- open cars in warm weather and closed cars in cold weather. The company converted to one-man operation of cars from 1928 onward.

In 1899, the company was acquired by the International Traction Company and together they were merged with others into the International Railway Company in 1902. Thereafter, this enterprise operated as I.R.C.'s Park & River Division.

Niagara Gorge Railroad Company:

Following organization of railways for the purpose since 1886 and some false starts, the Niagara Falls & Lewiston Railroad Company (NF&L RR) opened initial service on the trolley line through the Gorge at water level on the American side of the Niagara River on August 25, 1895. Only 75 days after construction had commenced, an interim service was operated from Lewiston as far as the Buttery Rapids Elevator just north of the railroad bridges. In spite of difficult construction, the first five miles were built in only 4 months. In 1896, service was extended over the full 7.41-mile railway from Lewiston steamship dock to downtown Niagara Falls. In the City, the company obtained trackage rights over the local streetcar line to reach its downtown terminal.

The Niagara Gorge Railroad Company was chartered to succeed the NF&L RR, and it was taken into the International Railway Company; however, I.R.C. maintained it as a separate corporation.

Heavy mountain-railroad type of construction was employed the whole way. International Traction Company rebuilt the whole line in 1899 to high standards, and the line was rebuilt several more times and ultimately was double track over its entire length.

The separate Lewiston & Youngstown Frontier Railway Company (L&YF Ry) was leased by the Niagara Gorge Railroad beginning April 1, 1904, and the latter company initiated through service from Niagara Falls to Youngstown and Fort Niagara. The seven-mile trolley line, opened in 1896, carried freight -- carloads of fruit to the New York Central System interchange at Lewiston, and during World War II carloads of material which the US Army Quartermaster Corps distributed to Western New York military bases from Fort Niagara.

The Niagara Gorge Railroad was bought on September 1, 1924, by the Niagara Falls Power Company which tried in vain to merge it with its Niagara Junction Railway. The power company bought the International Theater in Niagara Falls and converted it to the "Great Gorge Route Terminal" ticket office and waiting room.

The Niagara Gorge Belt Line:

Between Niagara Falls, New York, and Clifton (now Niagara Falls), Ontario, the International Traction Company built the Upper Steel Arch Bridge, then the longest steel arch in the world, and known alternatively as the "Falls View Bridge" and the "Honeymoon Bridge". Opened on September 23, 1897, it replaced an older suspension bridge on the same site. The bridge carried two tracks for streetcars. On July 1, 1898, the tracks were connected into I.R.C.'s Niagara Falls (New York) street railway system. A Bridge Street local service was provided between I.R.C.'s terminal and the Park & River division's Bridge Street station where it met local streetcars and interurbans of the Niagara, St.Catharines & Toronto Railway (NS&T). NS&T excursion trains from St.Catharines reached the I.R.C. "Great Gorge" terminal over the bridge.

"Great Gorge Route" sightseeing trips were

HISTORY

run from the Great Gorge Terminal, and "Canadian Scenic Route" trips began operating from the terminal via the bridge to the Falls and to Queenston.

I.R.C. dismantled the Niagara Falls-Clifton suspension bridge that it had replaced with the Falls View Bridge and re-erected it between Lewiston and Queenston as the Lower Suspension Bridge (or "Lewiston-Queenston Bridge"). Opened on July 21, 1899, it contained a single track for trolleys. The track connected with the Niagara Gorge Railroad on the New York end and the Park & River Division built a connecting track from Queenston to the bridge at the Ontario end. This final link enabled operation of a circular tour over both the Canadian Scenic Route and the Great Gorge Route.

In 1899, 18.9-mile circle tours, under the "Niagara Gorge Belt Line" banner, began operating clockwise around the loop. Cars ran every fifteen minutes during the summer season. The designated starting point was the I.R.C. terminal in Niagara Falls, New York, but passengers could begin at any of the stations along the way. A stop-over privilege allowed ticket-holders to linger at many of the sights and attractions and board a later trolley to continue their journeys. A passenger who remained with the car he or she boarded, could complete the circuit in two hours.

Interspersed among the regularly-scheduled Belt Line cars were the numerous regular cars to Chippewa, the Bridge Street locals, regular cars to Fort Niagara, local cars going to the Queenston and Lewiston steamship docks, tour groups' cars, I.R.C. specials from Buffalo direct to the Gorge, NS&T excursion trains, the Buffalo-to-steamship docks cars, occasional freight trains, and extra Belt Line cars added when the level of riding was high. All in all, it was a very busy railway. The Belt Line alone carried 17,000 passengers on its peak day. Two-car trains were often operated, and motored cars frequently pulled trailer cars.

The following pages take you on a "Niagara Gorge Belt Line" journey by way of a series of photographs. Let's take a ride …

On Falls Street in Niagara Falls, New York, closed car 29 and three open trailers await passengers for their spectacular journey to view awe-inspiring Niagara Falls and the sensational Niagara Gorge. This run has extra capacity because it meets the steamships from Toronto.

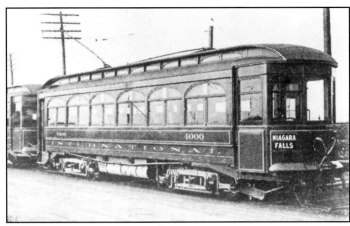

One of America's most successful street ventures was the Buffalo & Niagara Falls Electric Railway which began service between the two cities of its title in 1895. Competing successfully with the New York Central and Erie railroads, it earned enough revenue to buy the older street railway systems of both Buffalo and Niagara Falls. Through successive mergers and acquisitions, it became owner of the popular Niagara Gorge Belt Line. For decades, it was the most popular way for visitors to reach Niagara Falls. Through service to the Gorge was operated in season over its tracks from downtown Buffalo. It was a particularly busy rail line during the 1901 Pan American Exposition in Buffalo's Delaware Park when frequent interurban trains took exposition visitors on a side trip to the Falls and the Gorge from a special traction terminal at the grounds. The entire 20-mile run was in city streets although the tracks were located at the side of the pavement for much of the way.

Approaching the Falls from the Canadian side was enhanced when a short-line steam railroad was electrified in 1900 as the Niagara, St. Catharines & Toronto Railway. Interurban trolleys ran from St. Catharines and met the Niagara Gorge Belt Line cars at Bridge Street in Niagara Falls, Ontario. A terminal closer to the Falls was added in 1928 when NS&T built a rapid-transit quality line down the bluff. Belt Line cars passed in front of the attractive Tower Inn Terminal which was displaced in 1940 by a leg of the Queen Elizabeth Way that usurped the rapid transit right-of-way. Interurban cars continued to use the older Bridge Street terminal. NS&T outlasted the other electric traction operations in the Niagara Falls area, ending in 1947. The NS&T cars carried passengers between the Falls attractions and Port Dalhousie, immediately northwest of St. Catharines where steamships called from Toronto. Here, an interurban from St. Catharines in special service waits behind the terminal. Notice the Gray Coach Lines (a subsidiary of the Toronto Transit Commission) bus in the background.

In 1918, the International Railway Company (I.R.C.), successor to the Buffalo & Niagara Falls Electric Railway, completed its Buffalo-Niagara Falls High-Speed Line from the north neighborhoods of Buffalo to the eastern edge of Niagara Falls, providing a time-saving trip compared to the earlier line which continued as "the Old Line" until 1922 when it was severed between Gratwick (in North Tonawanda) and Cayuga Creek (in LaSalle, a separate city that was subsequently merged into Niagara Falls). The High-Speed Line with its direct routing on private right-of-way and full grade-separation from most streets in the cities of Tonawanda and North Tonawanda, was a forerunner of rapid transit. Special excursions by other interurban railways ran over these tracks or exchanged passengers with the I.R.C. under package tours from Rochester and Erie. The Gorge trolley was always a feature of these excursions. I.R.C. downgraded service on the High-Speed Line about the same time the Gorge Route ended, and discontinued service entirely in 1937. Here, high-speed car 2016 for Niagara Falls meets an interurban from Lockport near Main Street, Buffalo.

The steam railroads brought tourists from distant places. On the United States side regular train service was offered by the New York Central System, the Erie Railroad, and the Lehigh Valley Railroad, as well as other systems that operated pool service with these roads. In Canada, the Grand Trunk (Canadian National), and Michigan Central (New York Central) brought tourists to the Falls. Michigan Central even maintained a special station, Falls View, where trains stopped to allow passengers to view Horseshoe Falls from the heights, as seen in this postcard view. These and other railroads operated special excursion trains from distant places with competitively-priced tickets, often including the Niagara Gorge Belt Line ride in the package.

above: Canada Steamship Lines steamer *Chippewa* at Lewiston Dock one day in 1920. The *Chippewa* was built in 1894, and entered Toronto-Queenston/Lewiston service in 1896 to replace the *Cibola* which burned at the Lewiston dock in 1895.

above: In 1957, Cayuga Steamship Lines' steamer *Cayuga* is seen passing Niagara-on-the-Lake. The *Cayuga* was built in 1907 for this service.

The Belt Line cars served lower Niagara River docks at both Queenston on the Canadian side and Lewiston on the U.S. side. Canada Steamship Lines operated regular service to these points from Toronto. Although in Lewiston, a passenger might opt to use the Rome, Watertown & Ogdensburgh (of the New York Central System) steam train, nearly everyone availed themselves of the scenic trolley route through the Gorge to the Falls. This lake-boat service predated the electric cars (boats having connected at Queenston with the primitive Erie & Ontario Railway whose horsecars portaged passengers around the escarpment and falls to Chippewa beginning in 1839) and survived them until 1957. In addition, small steamships on the Niagara River from Buffalo landed at Slater's Dock near Chippewa to transfer passengers to local trolleys on the Park & River Division for the remainder of the trip to the Falls.

top:: The sidewheeler *Chippewa* enters Lake Ontario, passing the propeller Cayuga entering the mouth of the Niagara River.

above: *Chippewa* leaving Lewiston Dock and sailing north on the Niagara River, beginning its journey to Toronto, Ontario.

To carry steamship passengers and their luggage to and from the docks, starting in 1914, the International Railway Company operated combination car 733. From Buffalo, the car followed the old Falls Line via Gratwick, crossed the Niagara River at Niagara Falls into Canada, followed the Park & River Division along the top of the Gorge bluff, and descended the escarpment to Queenston Dock. Also, as needed, a pair of four-wheel baggage trailers were hauled by open cars to meet the steamboats.

Great Gorge Route open car 43 has just changed ends and is ready to take another load of tourists for a breath-taking trip along the Canadian rim of the Gorge and the United States shore of the Niagara River one day in 1935.

The Great Gorge Route Terminal migrated from time to time. A converted motion-picture theater served as waiting room at the advertised beginning of the Niagara Gorge Belt Line tour in Niagara Falls, New York, for part of the line's history. On October 27, 1925, a Gray Bus Line coach, built by Pierce-Arrow in Buffalo, awaits passengers for Lewiston and Youngstown by the direct highway route.

The Cataract House was a popular hotel and dining establishment until destroyed by fire in 1939. Behind the restaurant is the former International Theater serving as the Great Gorge Route ticket office and waiting room. Signs advertise connections for Toronto Steamers and for the night-time illumination trolley tour. From here, the Belt Line cars turned onto Riverway, and picked up additional passengers at the International Railway Terminal. I.R.C. erected this waiting room and carbarn on the site of the Tower Hotel which the Niagara Gorge Railroad purchased in 1900 and converted to a ticket office, waiting room, museum, restaurant, penny arcade, and gift shop. During 1903-1904, the 250-foot observation tower atop the hotel was sold, carefully disassembled, and re-erected by the American Wireless Telegraph Company at the Saint Louis World's Fair.

CANADIAN SCENIC ROUTE

After a block on Riverway, the Niagara Gorge Belt Line cars crossed the Niagara River below the Falls from Niagara Falls, New York, to Niagara Falls, Ontario. This iron arch Falls View Bridge was owned by International Railway Company; the 1,240-foot bridge's main span was 840 feet long. Its 37'7"-wide deck carried two tracks and a sidewalk each side of the roadway. Finished in 1896, the bridge's design and land allowed for eventual double-decking. Known as "Honeymoon Bridge", it was claimed to be the most-photographed bridge in the world. Trolleys crossed slowly 192 feet above the water to afford the rider "one of the grandest and most perfect views of the great cataracts obtainable." It collapsed under pressure of an ice floe on January 27, 1938, and was replaced by the present Rainbow Bridge in 1941.

On the Canadian side, Niagara Gorge Belt Line cars turned south, upriver, and headed for Table Rock House. Along the way on the Canadian bluff of the Gorge, passengers could alight at Clifton Incline Station and ride the inclined railway cars to the toe of the cliffs, there to board the famed Maid of the Mist boat through the churning waters and mist spray at the foot of the Falls. Car 49 awaits passengers sometime in 1932. The incline, built by Niagara Falls Park & River Railway in 1894, was under the sloped roof. The incline operated until 1991 and remains intact; boat passengers use new elevators. Notice the track switching off and leaving the right side of the picture; by a gradual ascent along the face of the cliffs, it provided access to a power plant in the Gorge. Clifton was the former name of Niagara Falls, Ontario.

The Niagara Gorge Belt Line cars continued south and turned just upstream from Table Rock House at the rim of the Canadian or Horseshoe Falls. Returning north, an I.R.C. trolley passes Clifton Incline Station again at the ornamental Mowat Gate entrance to Queen Victoria Park. The Horseshoe Falls form the background and one of the electric power generating stations is at river level to the right. At the left is Goat Island which separates the Canadian Falls from the American Falls farther left out of the picture. The side track to the power plant is blocked by timber to prevent runaway trolleys. Streetlights, added to the trolley guy poles in 1908, were later removed in favor of lights along the sidewalk, as in the next photograph.

CANADIAN SCENIC ROUTE

A postcard view of the Niagara Gorge Belt Line through Queen Victoria Park. In comparison with the picture below, the loss of attractive landscaping to the automobile can be appreciated. The Inspiration Point observation shelter appears at right overlooking the Gorge.

On September 11, 1932 — last day of service on the Canadian side -- car 679 passes the Refectory (left, out of the picture), built in 1903 to replace the Dufferin Cafe, a popular dining place to the present in Queen Victoria Park. The narrow level space between higher bluffs and the edge of the Gorge occasioned this stretch of single track. Beyond the stone wall is the deep Gorge immediately below the Falls. The distant buildings are in New York State.

Looking north from beneath the Michigan Central cantilever bridge past the Bridge Street station, this view shows the Grand Trunk bridge in the background and the Customs House to the right. The track arrangement allows the larger interurban cars to make the turns from and to Bridge Street off to the left beyond the station.

The I.R.C. Park & River Division station at Bridge Street, looking south toward the Michigan Central cantilever bridge. Connection was made here with cars of the Niagara, St. Catharines & Toronto Railway for St. Catharines, Port Dalhousie, and Toronto steamships.

CANADIAN SCENIC ROUTE

Just north of the Honeymoon Bridge, a southbound I.R.C. car has stopped to unload passengers after entering single track in Niagara Falls, Ontario. The Gorge is to the right.

A Niagara Gorge Belt Line car on River Street, Niagara Falls, Ontario, in 1900: Car 647 is one of the I.R.C. cars used in Belt Line service. Many of these 600-series open cars were rebuilt to closed cars and saw service in Lockport and Niagara Falls, New York, until 1937.

In 1892, the Niagara Park & River Railway bought the Whirlpool Rapids Incline. The railway cleaned up the property but kept the original buildings. The shed in the foreground was to protect visitors' carriages, but served as a shelter for trolley riders. The other building, a "curiosity" store, became the ticket office. This view shows fresh paint, before bold lettering was added -- "WHIRLPOOL RAPIDS" on the shelter, the store, and the fence behind the automobiles. This attraction continues today as "The Great Gorge Trip", but in 1934, elevators replaced the incline which had burned.

Barely visible atop the Gorge to the right is the Whirlpool Car House on the Canadian side. Destroyed by fire in 1904, it was never rebuilt. The line of white guy poles along the rim of the Gorge marks the course of the Niagara Gorge Belt Line tracks. The tracks at left are on the American side, rounding Whirlpool Point. The Grand Trunk bridge appears at the upper left.

After the fire destroyed I.R.C.'s Park & River Division car house, this small repair shop was erected. The frame building had pits for two cars and was equipped with lathe, emery wheel, drill press and other equipment. Outdoor storage capacity was for 30 cars. Cars 323 and 324 appear, and its stepwells identify one of the earlier observation.

A popular stop for the Niagara Gorge Belt Line trolley was Colt's Point station for the Spanish Aerocar. This viewcard, looking back from Thompson Point across the turbulent Whirlpool to the trolley station at Sinclair Point, shows the Great Gorge Route tracks at water level on the U.S. side (left in the picture). The Spanish Aerocar, a primitive aerial cableway, was opened in 1916 and continues in service. The Belt Line cars rounded a Horseshoe Curve around Saint David's Gorge -- the Whirlpool's basin -- crossing an iron trestle over the low spot -- Bowman Ravine -- and stopped at Thompson Point, the other end of the Spanish Aerocar. Thompson Point had been a station since 1897 when the railway built an observation platform there.

Aero Cable over Whirlpool Rapids, Niagara Falls

After Niagara Glen (opened to the public in 1896), the Niagara Gorge Belt Line cars continued north, serving the Sir Adam Beck Generating Station and concluding their trip along the rim of the Gorge 200 to 250 feet above the raging water at Sir Isaac Brock's Monument. The cars then descended the steep Niagara Escarpment. Open car 684 has begun the descent. In the middleground are the tracks (discernible by the white guy poles) of the same line having turned on a hairpin curve, and the village of Queenston immediately beyond. In the background is the lower Niagara River flowing to Lake Ontario with a steamship at Lewiston dock on the U.S. side. The Niagara Glen station ("Niagara Glen Inn" after 1923) remains in place as a snack bar.

In this 1900 view, open car 650 is leaning into the hairpin curve midway down the slope which dropped 5.7 feet in every 100 feet, with 185-foot Brock's Monument appearing in the upper left. The line was relocated and the curve widened following a tragic accident on July 7, 1915. A runaway car left the track at the sharp curve. In 1916, The rebuilt line was tested by setting a car without brakes free to coast successfully to the bottom without derailing.

The Niagara Gorge Belt Line cars passed the village of Queenston, then turned abruptly upriver to reach the Lewiston-Queenston Bridge at the toe of the escarpment. Some cars instead went through the village to the Queenston Dock. In 1920, part of the line down the escarpment was further relocated, this time to accommodate construction trains for the Sir Adam Beck electric power generating station a short distance upstream from the Lewiston-Queenston Bridge. Then, again, during 1928, the public road to the bridge was relocated and widened. Here can be seen the new roadbed crossing the the trolley track to reach the bridge in the background. Between this track and the river can be seen the double track of the Hydro Electric project.

On the Canadian side at Queenston, the I.R.C. single track curves past the Customs House. Looking west on July 3, 1928, some of the construction for road widening can be seen, as well as a Mack dump truck.

Looking across the Lewiston-Queenston Bridge from Canada to the U.S.: Built on the site of an earlier bridge blown down in an 1864 wind storm, this suspension bridge was officially known as the Lower Suspension Bridge. It was built by I.R.C. in 1899 with components from the Falls View Suspension Bridge which I.R.C. replaced during 1897-99 with the steel-arch Honeymoon Bridge, was 857 feet long, and contained a 28-foot wide deck with one trolley track in the roadway. It was of sufficient strength to hold at one time a 30-ton trolley every 400 feet and two continuous lines of automobiles. Although the bridge was removed about 1963, the stone towers in the background remain in place, incorporated into an Artpark "sculpture".

The Custom House on the Canadian side of the Lewiston-Queenston Bridge with an I.R.C. 500-series closed-type car awaiting customs and immigration clearance. The Customs House was owned by I.R.C.

LEWISTON-QUEENSTON BRIDGE

An early view of the Lewiston-Queenston Suspension Bridge shows the Customs House on the Canadian side and Brock's Monument above. This bridge marked the practical end of navigation in the swift Niagara River. The Escarpment here is where the great Falls began 123 centuries ago to carve the magnificent Gorge to the present location of Niagara Falls. The open trolley is running the Niagara Gorge Belt Line service.

This more recent view of the Lewiston-Queenston Suspension Bridge, looking toward Canada, shows the village of Queenston at the bottom of the Niagara Escarpment. The Hydro Electric generating plant access tracks pass under the bridge on the far shore. These tracks reached the Michigan Central Railroad that ran between Niagara-on-the-Lake and Fort Erie, opposite Buffalo; the major length of that line was the former Erie & Ontario Railway horse railway.

The Lewiston-Queenston Bridge in 1902 with an I.R.C. open car crossing from Ontario (left) to New York (right). Behind the trees on the right, the car will turn north on the road atop the stone wall. The trolley/boat terminal at Queenston appears behind the bridge's cables at the left. The Great Gorge Route trolley line shows briefly through the trees at the right below the bridge. The bridge replaced a Queenston-Lewiston ferry.

LEWISTON-QUEENSTON BRIDGE

The U.S. Customs House on the American side of the Lewiston-Queenston Bridge. The wood plank floor of the bridge shows clearly with the single trolley track. The section of the bridge in the immediate foreground spans the Great Gorge Route tracks.

I.R.C. car 508 has just arrived at the U.S. Customs House at the east end of the Lewiston-Queenston Bridge. This and the Custom House on the Canadian side, as well as those at both ends of the Honeymoon Bridge, were owned by I.R.C.

After crossing the Lewiston-Queenston Bridge and clearing Customs, the Niagara Gorge Belt Line cars continued north on the single track in the bridge-approach road to this point where they switched onto the tracks of the Niagara Gorge Railroad -- or "The Great Gorge Route". The advertised trip continued downstream to the village of Lewiston where the cars turned on a loop. But, some cars merely changed ends beyond the switch and went directly into the Gorge. The toe of the Niagara Escarpment is at the right. The then-new road in this 1928 scene is now buried under tons of rock spilled during construction of the Niagara Power Authority project in the 1950s.

The camera of Russell H. Shapley caught Great Gorge Route closed car 29 at the Lewiston steamship docks one day in 1932. The New York Central station is behind the car. Car 29 is typical of her series.

GREAT GORGE ROUTE

A postcard view of car 27 in front of the venerable Frontier House. Opened in 1824, guests included General Marquis de Lafayette, Louis Kossuth, Henry Clay, Daniel Webster, two Napoleons, and Jenny Lind. James Fenimore Cooper wrote "The Spy" here. This well preserved building continues in public service as one of the nation's finest-architected McDonald's restaurants, at 450 Center Street, Lewiston.

Two forces of nature menaced the line, but its income was sufficient to cover the cost of regular repairs. In winter, ice floes often rode up over the river banks, sheared the trolley guy poles, and distorted the track. Repairs to such damage were made rapidly. However, each spring, as the frozen ground thawed, the loose talus was dislodged from the Gorge walls and spilled onto the track bed. Each year, following the thaw, the railway shut down for the months of March and April to clear the tracks. In this view, work is under way to remove the loose talus from the land side and dump it on the water side. With the slump in revenue, the rock slide in 1935 was regarded by management as not worth the usual cost of the regular "spring cleaning". In earlier years, such a spill would have been cleared.

The Giant Rock was popular with photographers. It is a piece of the hard rock of the Gorge rim that fell long ago to lodge in the river bank. Because of its picturesqueness, Gorge Route engineers decided not to blast it out of the way. Today, the tracks are gone but the Giant Rock remains. Notice how the trolley wire was suspended from wood poles at the river side of the tracks and bolts in the rock of the Gorge wall. Notice, too, the wood guardrail that ran the entire length of the water-side track on the ends of its ties to avert a tragic plunge into the seething river. (Similar guardrails were installed on the outer track atop the Gorge on the Canadian side to keep derailed cars from plummeting into the canyon.) This tidy photograph, evidently taken shortly after completion of construction, served as a standard for subsequent illustrations of the Rock.

A postcard view of the Giant Rock with southbound car 6. The scene is later than the one above as indicated by some vegetation having taken hold. And, the wood guard rail was replaced by a guardrail of surplus rails. (See also the centerfold.)

Great Gorge Route : The Giant Rock, Niagara Falls

GREAT GORGE ROUTE

On the hot mid-day of August 5, 1927, a southbound 15-bench open car rounds the bend of Whirlpool Point on the U.S. side of the Gorge at the Niagara River's entrance to the surging Whirlpool, about three-quarters of the way along the spectacular Niagara Gorge Belt Line trolley tour. The Canadian cliffs are in the background.

The most exciting part of the ride was passing the Whirlpool Rapids. In the previous photograph, the car is at the entrance to the Whirlpool Rapids part of the Gorge. Here, just south of the Whirlpool, northbound open car 7 poses for its picture with the pair of railroad bridges in the background. Notice that the guardrail on the water-side track in this 1925 picture is located as in standard railroad practice.

Rounding the bend in the background of the photograph above, open car 9 heads south toward Niagara Falls in the early 1900s.

Car 5 heads north around the bend along the Whirlpool Rapids with the railroad bridges in the background. A train is silhouetted on the double-deck Grand Trunk bridge. Two types of guardrail protect the cars on this tight curve.

On a June morning in 1929, closed car 24 pauses next to the frothing river, south of the bend in the previous picture, for minor repairs to track drainage.

Park & River Division 15-bench open car 677 slows in its southbound journey for the Whirlpool Rapids stop on the balmy afternoon of June 15, 1927. Another car waits at the distant siding. Beyond is the Rapids View stop beneath the pair of railroad bridges. Atop the slope on the Canadian shore the trolley guy poles of the Canadian Scenic Route appear in silhouette. Thirty-two years after the Gorge Route was opened and eight years before it closed, this was a good year as evidenced by the tidy trackbeds. But, already some of the River's fury had been tamed by diversion of water to numerous hydro-electric power plants. Notice the fixed floodlights alongside the track at the bottom of the picture; others are situated each side of the Whirlpool Rapids station.

From the Gorge walk on the Canadian side – an attraction now called "The Great Gorge Trip" -- the churning Niagara River is most impressive in both sight and sound. People are strolling the boardwalk Promenade on the Canadian side and passengers are alighting from the trolley on the U.S. side to see the Giant Wave. The fury of the river throws the water a reported 30 to 40 feet into the air. The diversion of much of Niagara's water through huge hydro-electric power plants on both sides of the river have diminished the flow of water to the extent that the large wave has been tamed to less than half its former height. But, it is still impressive.

Open car 8's crew poses for a portrait while waiting for passengers to return up the stairway from the viewing platform at water level in the Gorge. These gentlemen are Bill Creighton on the car, Louis Eimer in the white coat, and Joe Childs at the corner of the car. Bill Piper is seated farther back in the car.

Passengers at one of the Gorge stops hurrying to the waters' edge to be awe-struck by the power and energy of the rushing river. Southbound open car 41's conductor watches over them.

A postcard view shows the big wave putting on its incessant performance while a Grand Trunk bridge-shuttle train crosses the upper deck of that railroad's steel arch bridge which replaced an earlier suspension bridge built by predecessor Great Western Railway. Behind it can be seen the Michigan Central's cantilever bridge which was also replaced subsequently (in 1925) by a stronger steel arch bridge and sold to a railroad in South Africa. The United States is to the left and in the background, while Canada is at the right.

SITE OF KIENUKA INDIAN VILLAGE

FRONTIER HOUSE INN? WHERE J. FENIMORE COOPER WROTE LEATHER STOCKING TALES

HERE STOOD FIRST OF 11 BLOCK HOUSES BUILT ON PORTAGE TRAIL

SITE OF FT. GRAY 1812

BLOCK HOUSE ON PORTAGE TRAIL

LEWISTON, U.S.A. BURNED 1813

7 MILES TO HISTORIC FORT NIAGARA

HERE STOOD MAGAZINE ROYAL ERECTED 1719

SITE OF OLD LEWISTON INCLINE 1764 FIRST RAILROAD BUILT ON THIS CONTINENT

TORONTO STEAMER LANDINGS

LAURA SECORD MEMORIAL

BATTLE OF QUEENSTON HEIGHTS OCT. 13, 1812

QUEENSTON CANADA

7 MILES TO HISTORIC FORT MISSISSAUGA OR FORT GEORGE

HOME OF FIRST NEWSPAPER IN UPPER CANADA 1792

GENERAL BROCK KILLED OCT. 13, 1812

OLD SHORE LINE OF LAKE ONTARIO

NIAGARA'S GR[E]
GORE TRI[P]
The FALLS and WHIRLPOOL RAPIDS
There is no Automobile
through the Gorge

The Whitney-Graham Co., Buffalo & New York

© 1930

5104. Giant Rock in the Gorge, Niagara.

Above: This panoramic view of the Niagara Gorge Belt Line, from a brochure in the collection of Albert D. Kerr, is one of many issued over the years by the cooperating I.R.C. Park & River Division and the Niagara Gorge Railroad. This 1932 edition is reproduced here at about three-quarters its original size.

Left: Postcard: "5104. Giant Rock in the Gorge, Niagara." Compare this view with the earlier photograph of Giant Rock to see some of the postcard printer's 'license'. The whitecaps on the waves, the trees, overhanging branches, and shadows reveal that this is exactly the same scene. But, an artist has removed the trolley wire and added a trolley car.

NIAGARA FALLS
U.S.A.

SITE OF BLOCK HOUSE
ON OLD PORTAGE
TRAIL

FORMERLY CALLED
MANCHESTER
BURNED IN 1813

SITE OF BLOCK HOUSE
ON OLD PORTAGE
TRAIL

GORGE
ROUTE
TERMINALS

FATHER HENNEPIN
FIRST EYE WITNESS
TO DESCRIBE
NIAGARA FALLS

HERE STOOD LAST
OF BLOCK HOUSES
ON PORTAGE TRAIL

167 FT.

FALLS VIEW
BRIDGE

NIAGARA FALLS
CANADA

BLONDIN WALKED
TIGHT ROPE
ACROSS GORGE
JUNE 30, 1859

8:—ELECTRIC LINE THROUGH THE GREAT GORGE, NIAGARA FALLS.

Right: From the collection of Richard A. Olday is a rare hand-colored season's greeting card that accompanied the distribution of annual passes in 1925. Niagara Gorge Railroad Company President A. H. Schoelkopf furnished free annual passes to local dignitaries, tour guides and travel agencies.

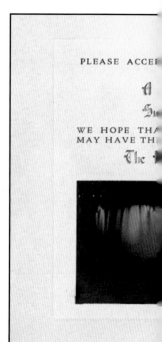

PLEASE ACCE

WE HOPE THA
MAY HAVE TH

The

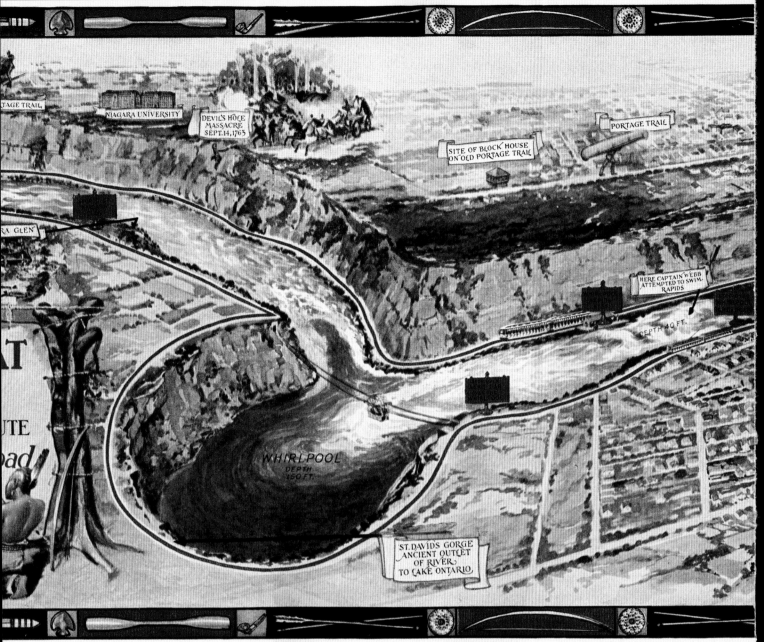

Whirlpool Rapids and Great Gorge Route, Niagara Falls

Left: Postcard: "Whirlpool Rapids and Great Gorge Route, Niagara Falls" The original wood guardrail, the Niagara Gorge Belt Line Station at Whirlpool Rapids and the railroad bridges show. On the Canadian side is the Promenade boardwalk. At the trolley station can be seen the stone stairway down to the flat water-level viewing area from which vantage point the "big wave" was best appreciated.

Right: Postcard "228: – Electric Line Through the Great Gorge, Niagara Falls." The U.S. end of the cantilever bridge is at the extreme left of this view of The Great Gorge Route climbing up the east Gorge wall to Niagara Falls, New York. This scene is before the line was double tracked and the gradient slope was eased.

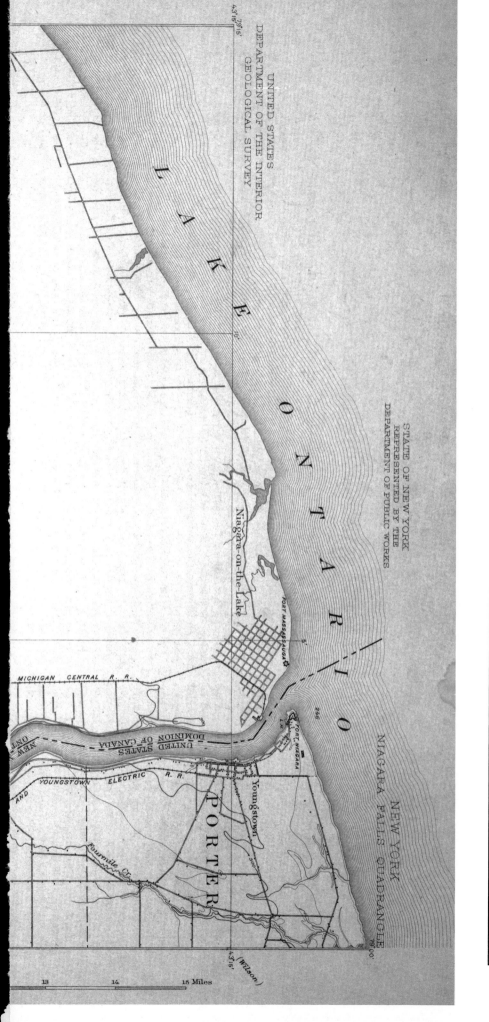

→ A Niagara Gorge Railroad Winter timetable from the *Official Interstate Guide (Succeeding the Official Guide of the Niagara Frontier) Trolley, Steamship and Railway Time Tables, Vol. 5, No. 12, December 1915.* In the Summer, Belt Line cars ran every 15 minutes.

← A section of the U.S. Geological Survey 15-minute quadrangle, "Niagara Falls," edition of March 1901. The map was surveyed, plotted, and drawn by the U.S. Lake Survey during 1893-1900 in cooperation with the State of New York. It is at the scale of 1:62,500 (approximately one inch equals one mile). Detail in Canada is not complete. Highlighted are the entireties of the Niagara Falls Park & River Railway, the Niagara Falls & Lewiston Electric Railway, and the Lewiston & Youngstown [Frontier] Railway from Slater's Dock at the south to Fort Niagara on the north. The Niagara Junction Railway appears as the Niagara Construction Company R.R. A portion of the Rome, Watertown & Ogdensburg north of Lewiston had already been dismantled. The two links between the Park & River trackage and the Michigan Central had not yet been built, nor was the branch between Youngstown and Fort Niagara Beach.

NIAGARA GORGE RAILROAD

Schedule Effective October 25th, 1914

LOCAL TIME TABLE

Subject to change without notice.

NORTH BOUND

	*1	*3	*5	*7	*9	*11	*15	*17	*19
	O	O	O	O	O	O	O		
Niagara Falls, Lv.	7.35	10.00	11.00	12.25	1.20	3.30	5.30		8.30
N.Y.C. Sta. "	7.38	10.03	11.03	12.28	1.23	3.33	5.33	6.40	8.33
Whirlpool Rapids "	7.53	10.15	11.15	12.40	1.35	3.45	5.45	6.43	8.45
Lewiston "	8.10	10.35	11.35	1.00	1.55	4.05	6.05	6.55	9.05
Stella Niagara "	8.20	10.43	11.43	1.08	2.03	4.13	6.13	7.20	9.13
Youngstown. "	8.27	10.51	11.51	1.16	2.11	4.21	6.21	7.58	9.21
Fort Niagara. Ar.	8.35	10.57	11.57	1.22	2.17	4.27	6.27	8.15	9.27

SOUTH BOUND

	*2	*4	*6	*8	*10	*12	*14	*16
		O	O	O	O	O	O	O
Fort Niagara. Lv		7.25	8.40	11.10	12.10	2.25	4.30	7.20
Youngstown. "		7.28	8.42	11.13	12.13	2.28	4.33	7.23
Stella Niagara "		7.42	8.57	11.27	12.27	2.42	4.47	7.37
Lewiston "	6.50	7.52	9.05	11.35	12.35	2.50	4.55	7.45
Whirlpool Rapids "	7.10	8.10	9.20	11.50	12.48	3.08	5.10	7.58
N.Y.C. Station "	7.28	8.27	9.40	12.10	1.10	3.30	5.30	8.15
Niagara Falls. Ar.	7.35	8.30	9.45	12.15	1.15	3.30	5.30	8.20

Additional cars leave Lewiston, N.Y. for Niagara Falls as follows:—9.35, 10.35 a.m. and every forty minutes up to and including 5.55 p.m.

Belt Line Cars leave Niagara Falls via Canadian side, 8.40 a. m. and every forty minutes up to and including 4.40 P. m.

·*Daily. (O) Baggage and Express except daily except Sunday. Time after 12.00 o'clock indicated by heavy type.

Southbound open car 49 waits for both passengers and crew on July 19, 1927, at one of the viewing stops along the Gorge. Windshields were undoubtedly added to these open cars to protect the motormen from the spray.

The original 910-foot Michigan Central cantilever railroad bridge frames the Suspension Bridge stop on the Niagara Gorge Belt Line trip. The height of the bridge deck, 220 feet above the water gives an impression of the depth of the unseen canyon below water level; the River is 215 feet here. Through the girders can be seen the Great Western's double-deck steel arch bridge. The upper deck carried a pair of railroad tracks; the lower deck was for wagons and automobiles. The suspension bridge that it replaced gave its name to the City of Suspension Bridge which was later merged into the City of Niagara Falls. An inclined railway, one of many in the Gorge, linked the water-level trolley station to street level above between the two railroad bridges and convenient to the union railroad station and the Niagara Falls local streetcar lines. The steel girder span in the Gorge replaces wood trestle-work that had washed out. Washouts at this point, one particularly tragic one during World War I, led to relocation of The Great Gorge Route tracks to a new shelf cut higher in the cliff; a remnant of the old roadbed became a viewing area reached by stone steps from the trolley line. The incline was discontinued about the same time.

After southbound cars (running clockwise around the Belt Line) passed under the railroad bridges, they gradually climbed the face of the Gorge wall to the rim (see centerfold). At the top, they passed the small Falls View carbarn and storage area, went under the New York Central's Niagara Branch tracks, and came up on the inland side of those tracks. Closed car 28 runs alongside the Central's tracks heading for downtown Niagara Falls. It will soon stop to allow passengers to tour the Schoellkopf Power Plant, then turn onto Walnut Street and follow 2nd Street, Main Street, 2nd Street again, serve the New York Central Depot, then head down Falls Street to the terminal, completing a most enjoyable circuit.

Special Illumination Trip: A contemporary pamphlet says, "Lest the darkness might hide the splendor of Niagara Falls, man has drenched the cataracts with brilliant floods of light and color. Special electric observation cars leave the terminals at dusk on summer evenings to take you down deep into the Gorge, where special lighting makes the rushing rapids sparkle in gleaming contrast to the black rock walls. Then the cars climb back to take you across Falls View Bridge and up to the Horseshoe, close to the great battery of lamps which throw 1,320,000,000 candle power of light upon the Falls. A stop-over provides time to enjoy the brilliant, colorful spectacle. No other trip at Niagara includes the Whirlpool Rapids Illumination." The famous Illumination Car is at the Niagara Gorge Railroad's Falls View carbarn in Niagara Falls, New York, on August 7, 1927. Short sidings throughout the Whirlpool Rapids Gorge enabled this little car to get out of the way of moving passenger cars while it swept the waves and spray with its arc light. The Falls, themselves, continue to be bathed in colored lights summer and winter, but since the demise of the trolley line, no one sees the night spectacle in the Gorge anymore. The searchlight car figured in many rescues from the churning river.

PARK & RIVER DIVISION

The Niagara Gorge Belt Line had some interesting appendages. At the south, from Table Rock House, Park & River Division trolleys continued upstream along the Canadian bank of the Niagara River, passing the traction system's power house, the Dufferin Islands, and Burning Springs, to the Welland River at the village of Chippewa. For a while, cars also continued from Chippewa to Slater's dock to meet boats from Buffalo. There were several significant bridges along the way to Chippewa. Dufferin Island Bridge crossed the outlet from the Dufferin Islands landscaped ponds.

The next bridge contained two spans over the inlet to the Dufferin Islands ponds. Open car 11 crosses the Burning Springs Bridge.

Another view of the two-span Burning Springs Bridge shows that the sturdy structure was built locally by the Hamilton Bridge Company in nearby Hamilton, Ontario.

The northerly appendage was the independent but affiliated Lewiston & Youngstown Frontier Railway (L&YF), known as "The Old Fort Route". In Lewiston, it connected with the Niagara Gorge Belt Line and steamships at Lewiston Dock and closer to the center of the village it tapped the Rome, Watertown & Ogdensburgh Railroad. The L&YF Ry. carried passengers through a productive fruit belt to the village of Youngstown, New York, and Fort Niagara. In the fort grounds, a branch went to the barracks and another to Fort Niagara Beach on Lake Ontario. Great Gorge Route car 7 runs through Youngstown in the early 1900s. Notice the railroad-style baggage wagon.

The Niagara Gorge Railroad leased the L&YF. After passenger service to Youngstown was discontinued, the line continued to carry freight and the company was sold to the Youngstown Cold Storage Company in 1932. Express motor 34 switches cars at Youngstown. No. 34 was formerly Niagara Gorge Railroad No. 34 and was used on the line until 1937 when replaced by an ex-Delaware, Lackawanna & Western Railroad 0-4-0 steam locomotive.

LEWISTON & YOUNGSTOWN FRONTIER RAILWAY

L&YF Ry. Plymouth gas locomotive no. FNO2, which replaced the aging steam locomotive, pulls a short freight train across the front lawns of North 8th Street in Lewiston on its seven-mile journey over the former trolley line to Youngstown, New York.

Plymouth locomotive FNO2 is proceeding north under Lewiston's Center Street in July 1950. All service ended a short while later. The tunnel remains today, but is filled in.

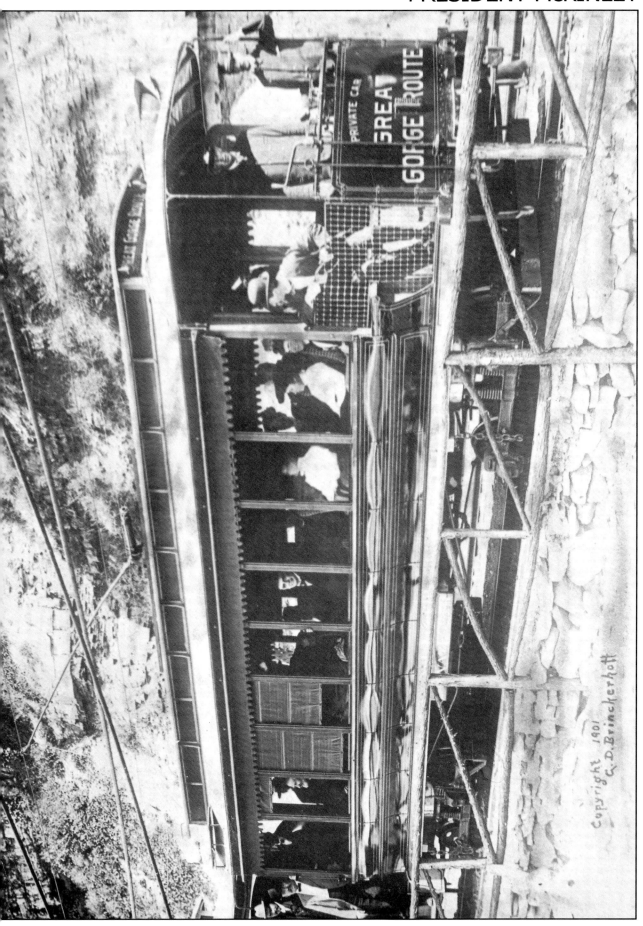

Copyright 1901
G.D.Brinckerhott

The Niagara Gorge Belt Line had a V.I.P. visitor on September 6, 1901, when President William McKinley enjoyed the ride from Lewiston (where he alighted from a special New York Central train) to Niagara Falls. His itinerary omitted the Canadian leg of the Belt Line inasmuch as to that time no U.S. President had ever set foot outside the United States. Afterwards, he hurried back to Buffalo to host a public reception at the Pan-American Exposition in Delaware Park. Among the throngs of people waiting to shake his hand was the assassin who shot the President. He died on September 14th at the home of the President of the Exposition, John G. Milburn. Vice President Theodore Roosevelt was inaugurated as President later the same day at the Wilcox Mansion on Delaware Avenue. In this photo, President McKinley appears in the fourth window from the right of this glistening Private Car. It can be seen that this special car was rebuilt from an open car; notice the flat floor without stepwells and the tell-tale form of the front bench. In addition, the maximum traction trucks, with large motored wheels and small idler wheels have been reversed from their usual position so that the larger wheels lead – undoubtedly to push debris off the rails.

43

PRINCE OF WALES VISIT

Another distinguished visitor to the Niagara Gorge Belt Line was His Royal Highness, the Prince of Wales (later Duke of Windsor), on September 10, 1927. His traveling party included his brother Prince George (then Prince of York and later King George VI), Great Britain Prime Minister Stanley Baldwin, Canadian Prime Minister W. L. MacKenzie King, U.S. Vice President Charles G. Dawes, Secretary of State Frank B. Kellogg, and other dignitaries. The occasion was the dedication of the new Peace Bridge across the Niagara River from Fort Erie, Ontario, to Buffalo, New York. The International Railway Company played host as seven especially-decorated trolleys began their trips at Chippewa, continued north over the Park & River Division to Queenston, over the Lower Suspension Bridge to Lewiston, south along the Niagara River on the Niagara Gorge Railroad to Niagara Falls, New York, over the Falls View Bridge to Niagara Falls, Ontario, then back to Chippewa. In an evident dress rehearsal on August 8, 1927, we see a lineup of the closed private car Ondiara, closed car 500, the convertible private car Rapids, and car 505 which had been outfitted as a private car, in Victoria Gardens with the Horseshoe Falls as a backdrop.

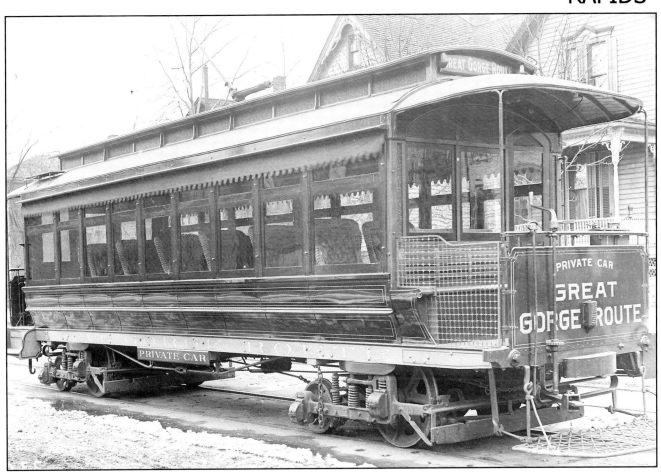

J. G. Brill Company of Philadelphia built a high-quality private car for the Niagara Gorge Railroad in 1895. It was furnished with carpeting and wicker chairs. This is the car that carried President McKinley. Here labeled only "PRIVATE CAR", it was named RAPIDS.

"RAPIDS"

Appearing later in gaudy paint and boldly named, a rebuilt and modernized RAPIDS poses with its spiffy crew at an overlook of the Falls near Table Rock House on August 8, 1927, ready for the Prince of Wales visit.

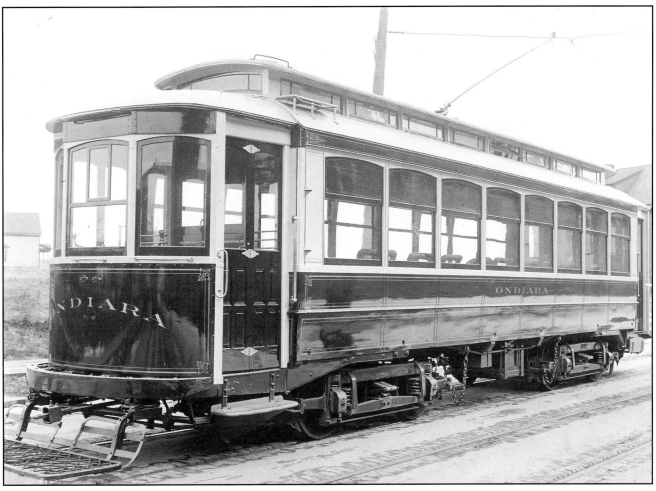

I.R.C. purchased this car from J. G. Brill Company in 1898 as a regular-service car for $15,187. Equipped with two Brill #27 trucks powered by four GE 57 50-horsepower motors, 42'6" long, and weighing 38,340 pounds, it was later rebuilt as the private car, ONDIARA, for use over the entire I.R.C. network. The interior was trimmed in mahogany and the car carried 24 wicker armchairs. It was outfitted with a toilet and washstand. ONDIARA was used for the Prince of Wales visit in 1927. "Ongiara" is the original Indian name for Niagara. The chairs survived for decades in the reception area of I.R.C.'s, Niagara Frontier Transit System's, and Niagara Frontier Transportation Authority's Cold Spring garage/shop offices.

CAR 505 AND "NIAGARA"

I.R.C. car 505 was especially converted to a private car for the Prince of Wales visit in 1927. This shows the interior with carpets and armchairs. See the tail car (left) in the photograph on the Prince of Wales page for the exterior appearance of car 505.

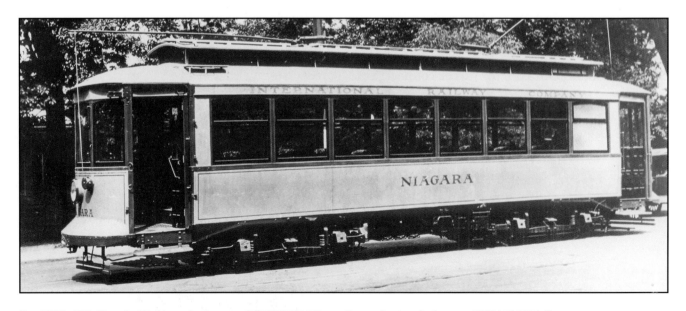

In 1930, I.R.C. rebuilt its private car "ONDIARA" as the private chair car "NIAGARA."

I.R.C. PARK & RIVER DIVISION ROSTER
INTERNATIONAL RAILWAY COMPANY PARK & RIVER DIVISION
CHIPPAWA to QUEENSTON, ONTARIO, CANADA
EQUIPMENT ROSTER, October 26, 1926

year	car no.	builder	type	length	weight	trucks	motors	notes
1892	32	Patterson & Corbin	line	17'6"		Brill single	GE800(2)	1
1894	722	J.G. Brill	closed	37'2"	42,460	Brill 27	40HP(4)	
1894	732	J.G. Brill	closed	37'2"	42,460	Brill 27	40HP(4)	
1894	733	J.G. Brill	closed	38'8"	42,460	Brill 27	40HP(4)	2
1894	737	J.G. Brill	closed	40'4"	44,120	Brill 27	40HP(4)	
1894	741	J.G. Brill	closed	40'4"	44,120	Brill 27	40HP(4)	
1894	746	J.G. Brill	closed	40'4"	44,120	Brill 27	40HP(4)	
1898	ONDIARA	J.G. Brill	closed	42'6"	38.340	Brill 27	50HP(4)	3
1900	E-2	Intl.Ry.Co.	flat	38'4"	44,650	Brill 27G	50HP(4)	4
1900	500	J.G. Brill	closed	44'0"	44,000	Brill 27-F	50HP(4)	6, 7
1900	501	J.G. Brill	closed	44'0"	44,000	Brill 27-F	50HP(4)	6, 7
1900	502	J.G. Brill	closed	44'0"	44,000	Brill 27-F	50HP(4)	6, 7
1900	504	J.G. Brill	closed	44'0"	44,000	Brill 27-F	50HP(4)	6, 7
1900	505	J.G. Brill	closed	44'0"	44,000	Brill 27-F	50HP(4)	6, 7
1900	650	J.G. Brill	open	42'8"	37,000	Brill 27	50HP(4)	
1900	651	J.G. Brill	open	42'8"	37,000	Brill 27	50HP(4)	
1900	652	J.G. Brill	open	42'8"	37,000	Brill 27	50HP(4)	
1900	653	J.G. Brill	open	42'8"	37,000	Brill 27	50HP(4)	
1900	655	J.G. Brill	open	42'8"	37,000	Brill 27	50HP(4)	
1900	656	J.G. Brill	open	43'0"	37,000	Brill 27	50HP(4)	
1900	659	J.G. Brill	open	43'0"	37,000	Brill 27	50HP(4)	
1900	668	J.G. Brill	open	43'0"	37,000	Brill 27	50HP(4)	
1900	670	J.G. Brill	open	43'0"	37,000	Brill 27	50HP(4)	
1900	673	J.G. Brill	open	42'8"	37,000	Brill 27	50HP(4)	
1900	677	J.G. Brill	open	42'8"	37,000	Brill 27	50HP(4)	
1900	678	J.G. Brill	open	42'8"	37,000	Brill 27	50HP(4)	
1900	679	J.G. Brill	open	42'8"	37,000	Brill 27	50HP(4)	
1900	682	J.G. Brill	open	43'0"	37,000	Brill 27	50HP(4)	
1900	684	J.G. Brill	open	43'0"	37,000	Brill 27	50HP(4)	8
1900	685	J.G. Brill	open	43'0"	37,000	Brill 27	50HP(4)	8
1900	686	J.G. Brill	open	42'8"	37,000	Brill 27	50HP(4)	
1900	687	J.G. Brill	open	42'8"	37,000	Brill 27	50HP(4)	

notes:

1. original closed car of Niagara Falls Park & River Railway

2. passenger and baggage car, not assigned to the Canadian Division but used between Buffalo and Queenston, Ontario, for direct connection to Toronto steamships from 1914 until 1932; rebuilt by I.R.C. in 1902

3 private chair car "Ondiara" was used over all I.R.C. lines, including visit by Prince of Wales over entire Niagara Belt Line in 1927; car rebuilt to private chair car "Niagara" in 1930.

4. rebuilt 1910, 1911, 1913

6 originally open cars 689-693

7. rebuilt 1912 by International Railway Company

8. combination sweeper and 14-bench open car

Not included in the above roster are cars 600 through 649. These cars were transferred to city service in Niagara Falls (New York), Lockport, and Buffalo prior to the date of the roster. Some of these cars had already been rebuilt to closed cars in 1912, the remaining open cars were rebuilt to closed cars by the Kuhlman Car Company in Cleveland, Ohio. All were original open cars built by J. G. Brill in 1900 and came equipped with Brill 27 trucks. Conversion to city service entailed preparing the cars for one-man operation and replacing trucks on as many cars as possible with Brill 39E and 39E1 maximum traction trucks. Car 628 retained its Brill 27 trucks to retirement in 1938.

NIAGARA GORGE RAILROAD ROSTER

NIAGARA GORGE RAILROAD COMPANY - NIAGARA FALLS, NEW YORK, TO LEWISTON, NEW YORK
EQUIPMENT ROSTER

year	car no.	builder	type	length	weight	trucks	motors	notes
1895	RAPIDS	J. G. Brill	private			double		1
1907	27	G.C.Kuhlman	closed	40'1"		Brill 27-G1	40HP(4)	
1907	28	G.C.Kuhlman	closed	40'1"		Brill 27-G1	40HP(4)	
1907	29	G.C.Kuhlman	closed	40'1"		Brill 27-G1	40HP(4)	
1907	22	G.C.Kuhlman	open			single		2
1907	27	G.C.Kuhlman	open			single		2
1907	29	G.C.Kuhlman	open			single		2
1910	41	J.G. Brill	open	12-bench	double			
1910	42	J.G. Brill	open	12-bench	double			
1910	43	J.G. Brill	open	12-bench	double			
1910	44	J.G. Brill	open	12-bench	double			
1910	45	J.G. Brill	open	12-bench	double			
1910	46	J.G. Brill	open	12-bench	double			
1910	47	J.G. Brill	open	12-bench	double			
1910	48	J.G. Brill	open	12-bench	double			
1910	49	J.G. Brill	open	12-bench	double			
1910	54		open	10-bench		trailer		
1910	55		open	10-bench		trailer		
1910	56		open	10-bench		trailer		
1910	57		open	10-bench		trailer		
1910	58		open	10-bench		trailer		
1910	59		open	10-bench		trailer		
1910	60		open	10-bench		trailer		
1910	63		open	10-bench		trailer		
1910	64		open	10-bench		trailer		
1910	65		open	10-bench		trailer		
1910	66		open	10-bench		trailer		
1910	67		open	10-bench		trailer		
1910	69		open	10-bench		trailer		
1910	70		open	9-bench		trailer		
1910	71		open	9-bench		trailer		
1910	72		open	9-bench		trailer		
1910	73		open	9-bench		trailer		
1910	74		open	9-bench		trailer		
1910	75		open	9-bench		trailer		
1910	76		open	10-bench		trailer		
1910	77		open	10-bench		trailer		
1910	78		open	10-bench		trailer		
1910	79		open	10-bench		trailer		
1910	80		open	10-bench		trailer		
1910	61		express			single	trailer	
1910	62		express			single	trailer	
1915	1	J.G. Brill	open	12-bench	double			3
1915	2	J.G. Brill	open	12-bench	double			3
1915	3	J.G. Brill	open	12-bench	double			3
1915	4	J.G. Brill	open	12-bench	double			3
1915	5	J.G. Brill	open	12-bench	double			3
1915	6	J.G. Brill	open	12-bench	double			3
1915	7	J.G. Brill	open	12-bench	double			3
1915	8	J.G. Brill	open	12-bench	double			3
1915	9	J.G. Brill	open	12-bench	double			3
1915	10	J.G. Brill	open	12-bench	double			3
1915	11	J.G. Brill	open	12-bench	double			3
1915	12	J.G. Brill	open	12-bench	double			3
1915	13	J.G. Brill	open	12-bench	double			3
1915	14	J.G. Brill	open	12-bench	double			3
1915	15	J.G. Brill	open	12-bench	double			3
1915	16	J.G. Brill	open	12-bench	double			3
1915	17	J.G. Brill	open	12-bench	double			3
1915	18	J.G. Brill	open	12-bench	double			3
1915	19	J.G. Brill	closed			double		4
1915	20	J.G. Brill	closed			double		4
1915	23	J.G. Brill	closed			double		5
1915	24	J.G. Brill	closed			double		5
unk.	25	J.G. Brill	closed			double		6
unk.	26	J.G. Brill	closed			double		7
unk.	30		sweeper			single		
unk.	34		freight motor		double			8
unk.	84		express motor			double		9

notes:
1. furnished with wicker chairs and carpeting
2. ex-Lewiston & Youngstown Frontier Railway Company
3. some cars later rebuilt to closed
4. original Niagara Falls & Lewiston Railroad
5. ex-Cleveland, Ohio
6. No. 26 sold to Niagara Junction Railway Company in 1935, then to Warehouse Point, Connecticut trolley museum
7. ex-Morris County Traction Company (New Jersey)
8. to Lewiston & Youngstown Frontier Railway; used until 1937
9. to Niagara Junction Railway Company, as NJ T-2

This roster of rolling stock of the Niagara Gorge Railroad Company is incomplete due to the unavailability of records account destroyed by the railroad's owner; however, William R. Gordon's "90 Years of Buffalo Railways" continues to be a valuable reference.

BRILL'S MAGAZINE

PUBLISHED IN THE INTERESTS OF

The J. G. BRILL COMPANY, Philadelphia

AMERICAN CAR COMPANY, St. Louis   JOHN STEPHENSON COMPANY, Elizabeth
G. C. KUHLMAN COMPANY, Cleveland   WASON MANUFACTURING CO., Springfield

VOL. I.   JULY 15, 1907.   No. 7

Semi-Convertible Cars for the Niagara Gorge Railroad

The Niagara Gorge Railroad Company has recently put in operation a number of Brill Grooveless Post Semi-Convertible cars built by The G. C. Kuhlman Car Company. Just how well these cars have met the conditions at Niagara is best answered by quoting the following from a letter received from Mr. Bert L. Jones, general manager of the "Great Gorge Route," who has kindly furnished photographs and information.

"The semi-convertible cars purchased from you recently are giving absolutely perfect satisfaction and not a busy day passes that our superintendent does not speak enthusiastically of the efficiency of them. Our superintendent has always said that excursionists would not enter closed cars when open cars were in sight; but he informs me that these new semi-convertibles are, if anything, more popular than the open cars, as excursionists on leaving the boat at Lewiston, invariably take these cars in preference to all others. On July 1st, which was Dominion Day, the Niagara Navigation Company and the Turbine Steamship Company discharged at Lewiston in the forenoon, 4500 passengers ticketed over our line, and therefore we had a good opportunity to test these semi-convertibles, to each of which was attached three trailers. Our line being a short one (16 miles, and but 8 miles from the boat landing at Lewiston to Niagara Falls, whence the above passengers were routed) the four-train cars are able to make the trip to Niagara Falls and return to Lewiston in time for the next boat, as they come in usually about two hours apart, and therefore these trains made four round trips that forenoon, and in this way with our extra equipment, we were able to handle our passengers in the very best shape. We are therefore perfectly satisfied with our new cars and if they continue to give us satisfaction, will undoubtedly order more in the near future."

The Brill Semi-Convertible is peculiarly suited to scenic roads, not only because the large windows in no wise obstruct the range of vision, but also because of the assurance to passengers of protection from stormy weather and rapid fall of temperature in summer. The Niagara Gorge Railway in winter operates closed cars for tourists wishing to see Niagara in its winter garb, but the Semi-Convertible, of course, will be used throughout the year, thereby eliminating the double equipment.

The Semi-Convertibles for Niagara are of standard construction and plan for cars of that length, 30' 8"; other dimensions are as follows: Length over end panels, 30' 8"; over vestibules, 40' 1"; width over sills including sheathing, 7' 11½"; over posts at belt, 8' 2"; size of side sills, 4" x 7¾"; end sills, 5¼" x 6⅞"; sill plates, 15" x ⅜". Interiors are finished in cherry; ceilings of birch veneer. The cane seats are of Brill manufacture as are also the trucks which are the No. 27-G1 type with 4' 6" wheel base; four 40 h. p. motors are used per car.

CLOSED CARS

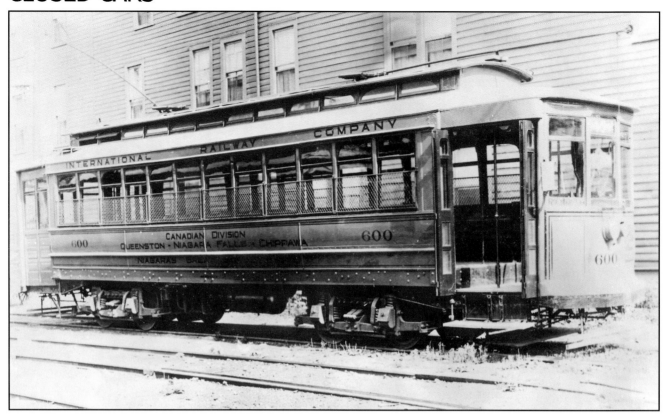

I.R.C. closed car 600 relaxes at the Niagara Falls, New York, car house. It was later rebuilt for city streetcar service in Buffalo. Unusual are its air-operated doors associated with one-man operation.

Car 19, reposing at the Niagara Falls car house, is representative of the semi-convertible fleet that sustained Niagara Gorge Belt Line service over a long period of years. Built by Brill for the Niagara Falls & Lewiston Railroad in 1915, she ran until the end of the Great Gorge Route twenty years later.

Builder's photo: Semiconvertible car 28 was designed by The J. G. Brill Company of Philadelphia, Pennsylvania, and built by an affiliate, G. C. Kuhlman Car Company, in Cleveland, Ohio. The car is mounted on No. 27-G1 trucks manufactured by the General Electric Company. (See the Niagara Gorge Railroad's testimonial statement about these cars in the accompanying article from Brill Magazine.)

Great Gorge Route closed car 28 on Main Street, Niagara Falls, New York.

CLOSED CARS

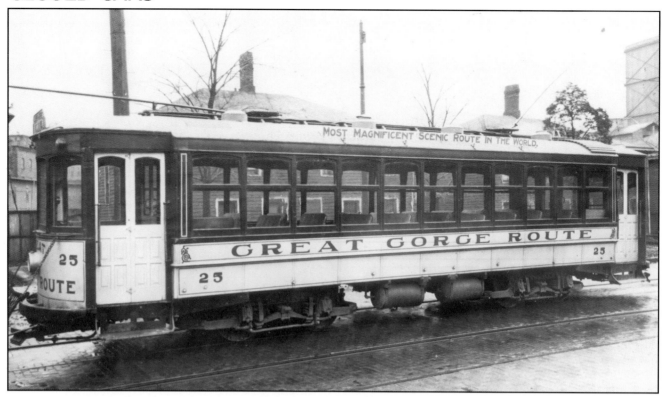

Closed car 25, rebuilt with an arch roof, continued in service until abandonment on September 17, 1935.

Great Gorge Route car 26, with arch roof, is signed for a tour group to the Toronto steamers, but has evidently had a mishap in traffic as evidenced by the damage to the side of the car.

Great Gorge Route deck-roof, twelve-bench, open motor car 12 is at the Falls View carbarn in Niagara Falls, New York. This is the type of car that was rebuilt as the private car, Rapids.

Not quite a twin to car 12, above, is trailer 80 with only ten benches, capable of carrying 50 seated passengers, posing at the Falls View carbarn.

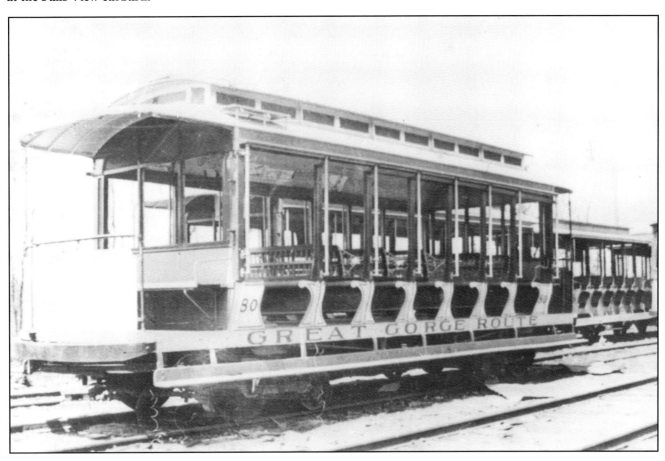

OPEN CARS

Railroad roof, fifteen-bench open car 47 represents the other type of open car used on Niagara's Great Gorge Trip. Here it is at the Falls View carbarn in Niagara Falls, New York, on March 10, 1927, evidently having spent the winter being readied for the coming summer season. The New York Central's tracks are on the embankment behind the car house.

The cars delivered by Brill to the Lewiston & Youngstown Frontier Railway were similar to cars delivered to the Niagara Gorge Railroad. This is the builder's official portrait of one of the twelve-bench cars.

Great Gorge Route snow-sweeper 30 at the Niagara Falls, New York, car house after abandonment in 1935.

Great Gorge Route car 84 was rebuilt as an express car and was subsequently sold in 1935 to the freight-only Niagara Junction Railway to become that railroad's T-2.

Niagara Junction Railway Company Track Department car T-2, former Great Gorge Route car 84, at Niagara Falls, New York.

The Niagara Junction Railway Line Department line car was formerly Niagara Gorge Railroad car 26. Sold to the Warehouse Point trolley museum in Connecticut, its trucks and electrical equipment were salvaged for the restoration of other cars.

The Niagara Gorge Railroad Company owned the Niagara Gray Bus Line, Inc, which operated bus service over local highways between Niagara Falls and Youngstown by way of Lewiston. Along with the trolleys, these buses met the steamships at Lewiston Dock. One of five similar buses that comprised the fleet, a Gray Bus Line bus, newly built by the Pierce-Arrow factory in Buffalo, poses for its portrait in 1924 next to the historic Adams Power Station. In 1936, I.R.C. bought this bus service which continued to be operated by successor Niagara Frontier Transit System, Inc. ("NFT"), but was eventually cut back from Youngstown to Lewiston. In later years, buses were another way to reach the popular Niagara Gorge Belt Line trolley trip. When the Grand Island bridges were finished in 1935, Van Dyke Sightseeing Company began running de luxe buses from Buffalo to Niagara Falls via this short route. This service was acquired by Grand Island Transit Corporation in 1938 and, in turn, by the Niagara Frontier Transportation Authority in 1974. Today's modern buses, using this short route need as many minutes between terminals as did the Buffalo-Niagara Falls High Speed Line interurban trolleys, even though the interurban cars could move in Buffalo only at city traffic speed between Court Street and the beginning of the private right-of-way near LaSalle Avenue. Following the end of trolley service in Canada, the Niagara Parks Commission awarded exclusive rights to serve the attractions to Highway King Coach Lines in 1933. Highway King affiliated with Gray Line Sightseeing Companies to benefit from its world-wide marketing, reputation, and requirement for authentic descriptions of the sights verified by historians. In 1938, Highway King became Canada Coach Lines, a wholly-owned subsidiary of the Hamilton Street Railway Company. Independent today, the bus company is known as Funtrek.

TOURS

Left: The Philadelphia Rapid Transit Company (PRT) and the International Railway Company (I.R.C.) were under the same management -- Mitten Management (Dr. Thomas E. Mitten of Philadelphia). The two distant systems were joined by a motor bus tour route using PRT and I.R.C. gas-electric parlor coaches "which are recognized as the last word in automotive engineering." The two-day ride from the City of Brotherly Love took the traveler to Delaware Water Gap for lunch, Binghamton for dinner and overnight stay, Watkins Glen for lunch, Batavia for dinner, and the Hotel Buffalo at Washington and Swan Streets. One day was devoted to an electric train ride on the High Speed Line to Niagara Falls, a trolley trip on the Niagara Gorge Belt Line, and return to Buffalo by the High Speed Line. Two more days took the passenger from the Queen City of the Lakes to Dansville, Williamsport for dinner and overnight lodging, Harrisburg for lunch, and PRT's Inter-City Motorbus Waiting Room and Ticket Office in Philadelphia -- all for $50.00 in 1926.

NIAGARA GORGE BELT LINE.
NIAGARA FALLS, N. Y.

Right: On the main attraction, each Niagara Gorge Belt Line rider was given a small "READ AS YOU RIDE" booklet which depicted and described 15 views from the car or other places to stop-over along the 18.9-mile, two-hour ride.

Sesqui-Centennial *Niagara Falls*

The American Wonderland

Via
Gas-Electric Motorbus
PRT
UNDER MITTEN MANAGEMENT

PRT
UNDER MITTEN MANAGEMENT

PHILADELPHIA BUFFALO

The Niagara Belt Line:

Here, reproduced facsimile, is the 1932 official description of the sights to be seen from the Niagara Gorge Belt Line cars. It includes fares and a list of ticket agencies:

THE NIAGARA BELT LINE
AROUND THE FALLS AND THROUGH THE FAMOUS GORGE

AS LIGHT IS REQUIRED to bring out the colors of the rainbow, so is a trip around the Niagara Belt Line necessary to bring out the true beauties and grandeur of the American and Horseshoe Falls, the great Whirlpool Rapids, the wonderful Gorge, and the magnificent scenery that has made Niagara world-famous. Before the great lines of electric traction were established at the Falls it was impossible to gain access to the many points of interest now reached with ease by the wonderful trolley system encircling the Gorge, which, for a distance of over twenty miles, continually presents to the tourist an ever-changing panorama of wonderful scenery. The scenic tour jointly arranged by the International Railway and the Niagara Gorge Railroad, the former operating the electric line

Niagara Belt Line Cars Crossing Upper Steel Arch Bridge

along the Canadian side of the river and the great bridges at Niagara Falls and Queenston; and the Niagara Gorge Railroad, or "Great Gorge Route," which follows through the Niagara canyon from Lewiston to the Falls along the water's edge, enables the traveler to make this wonderful ride at Niagara *without change of cars.*

Belt Line cars pass through Falls and Second streets in Niagara Falls, N. Y., convenient to all principal hotels and railway depots, or the passenger may begin the trip at the Terminal Station of the International Railway, fronting Prospect Park on Riverway (or at Soldiers' Monument), cars leaving at fifteen-minute intervals during the day in summer and every half-hour during winter season.

Boarding one of these observation cars, designated "Niagara Belt Line," the tourist is carried to the American approach of the great steel arch bridge spanning the Niagara River a few hundred feet below the Falls, and over this remarkable structure

1

THE NIAGARA BELT LINE
COVERING CANADIAN AND AMERICAN SIDES
A 20 MILE RIDE FOR $1.00 ROUND TRIP

Panoramic View of American and Horseshoe Falls, as seen from Niagara Belt Line Cars

to Canada. As the car slowly moves over the bridge, one of the grandest and most perfect views of the Falls is gradually unfolded, and in its course for nearly one mile up the river on the Canadian side this magnificent view of the American and Horseshoe Falls is ever present to the eye, always from a new point of vantage, until the car reaches Table Rock, almost at the brink of the Horseshoe Fall. Here the tourist may remain, if he so desires, continuing his journey on some later car. From this point may also be seen the Canadian rapids, above the Falls, and the wild and plunging waters in the mad rush before leaping into the chasm.

The Canadian electrical power plants are located here, affording many interesting and instructive features. At Table Rock the car describes a loop and returns down the Canadian side of the river toward Queenston, skirting the brink of the cliff for a distance of nine miles, always within plain view of the river and Gorge. On approaching the great Railway bridges (Michigan Central Cantilever and Grand Trunk Steel Arch), about two miles distant from the Falls, the placid waters of the lower river once more become turbulent until the wonderful Whirlpool Rapids is reached. Continuing along the high bank a splendid view of the great

Brock's Monument, 185 feet high, on Queenston Heights

2

THE NIAGARA BELT LINE

TICKETS ENTITLE PASSENGERS TO FREE STOP-OVER PRIVILEGES AT POINTS OF INTEREST

Whirlpool is obtained, and the course of the river at this point taking an abrupt turn, the quaint villages of Queenston and Lewiston loom into view and the river on its way to Lake Ontario may be seen for several miles. Continuing on and approaching Queenston Heights, a turn in the route suddenly reveals the magnificent panorama of the lower Niagara River and the surrounding country for miles to Lake Ontario. This fertile plateau, stretching for many miles along the south shore of the lake is one of the most productive fruit regions in America.

At Queenston Heights the visitor may see the great monument, 185 feet high, erected 1853 (rebuilt 1870), to the memory of the famous British General, Sir Isaac Brock, who fell in battle on these Heights in the War of 1812. A gradual and easy descent from the Heights brings the car to the approach of the Lewiston Suspension Bridge. Along the way and within a few feet

Passing Whirlpool Rapids

of the railway may be seen the cenotaph erected by the Prince of Wales (late King of England, Edward VII.) on his visit to this country in 1860, and marks the spot where General Brock fell. Here is the village of Queenston, with Lewiston across the river, these being the head of navigation of the lower Niagara River and the ports of call for steamers of the Niagara Navigation Co. to and from Toronto. Crossing the Suspension Bridge, the car proceeds to the village of Lewiston, where a short stay may be made to advantage. Here the return trip to Niagara Falls is commenced, over the "Great Gorge Route," running close to the water's edge nearly all the way. This ride up the Gorge is so wonderful in its scenic features as to defy description, the car passing on amid scenes of imposing grandeur by a winding course following the contour of the river bank. A short time after leaving Lewiston the Devil's Hole is passed. This spot is prominent in the annals of Niagara Frontier history, a British

3

THE NIAGARA BELT LINE

TICKETS MUST BE USED TO CONTINUE IN THE SAME DIRECTION

Entrance to the Gorge

caravan and a company of soldiers being ambushed and massacred by the Indians in 1763, the entire company being driven over the cliff to death, on the rocks below.

On the way up the Gorge a closer view of the great Whirlpool is obtained from the car, and at a turn in the river the Whirlpool Rapids suddenly looms into view, churning, foaming, tossing, and forming a scene that holds the tourist spellbound with amazement, admiration and awe. The Whirlpool Rapids is one of the most striking spectacles of the visit to Niagara. After leaving the Rapids and passing underneath the great railway bridges the car begins an easy ascent along the river bank, and here the river and all its beauties sink into restful dimness. Nearing the top a mass of natural stone formation is passed and once more the visitor is within the city of Niagara Falls and ready to alight at the railway station or hotel from which the journey was begun, after a ride *unequaled by any scenic tour in the world.*

Whirlpool Rapids as seen from the Niagara Belt Line Cars

4

THE NIAGARA BELT LINE

CARS OPERATED EVERY DAY IN THE YEAR AT FREQUENT INTERVALS

Niagara Belt Line cars carry signs as shown above

NIAGARA BELT LINE
Round Trip Fare, $1.00

The trolley cars making this delightful, interesting and instructive trip leave from the International Railway terminal (Riverway) and Niagara Gorge Railroad Office, 38 West Falls Street (opposite Prospect Park), every fifteen minutes from June 15th to Oct. 1st, and at frequent intervals the balance of the year.

Free stop-over privileges are allowed at all points of interest, principal among them being the Horseshoe Fall, Whirlpool View, Niagara Glen, Brock's Monument, Queenston (Canadian side), Lewiston and Whirlpool Rapids (American side).

This trip should be made to consume an entire day, although by continuous journey it may be covered in two hours' time.

Cars may also be boarded at the New York Central Station, or along the route in Niagara Falls.

☞ **Belt Line Cars are Operated Every Day in the Year**

POPULAR TRIPS
NIAGARA BELT LINE, INCLUDING FORT NIAGARA (American Side)
$1.25 Round Trip

Arriving at Lewiston, break the Belt Line journey and take trip to Youngstown, Fort Niagara and Fort Niagara Beach on Lake Ontario. Visit the Old Historic Fort where U. S. Government troops are permanently stationed. Secure tickets at Niagara Gorge R. R. Offices.

NIAGARA BELT LINE, INCLUDING CHIPPAWA (Canadian Side)
$1.25 Round Trip

From the Upper Steel Arch Bridge to Chippawa following along the Upper River, passing the great intakes and power houses, returning to Horseshoe Fall to resume Belt Line Trip. This ticket may be secured at the International Railway Offices.

Combination Ticket, $1.50 Round Trip

This ticket is sold by excursion agents on trains of the New York Central Lines entering Niagara Falls, and provides a carriage furnished by the Niagara Falls Transfer Co., which is taken from inside the station grounds, for a ride through the State Reservation and a trip on the Niagara Belt Line, around the Falls and through the famous Gorge. The carriage ride includes Prospect Park, Goat Island, Luna Island and the Three Sister Islands and returns you to the International Ry. terminal or the Niagara Gorge R. R. Office, from where the trip via electric car begins.

OF INTEREST TO TOURISTS

Height of American Falls, 167 ft.; contour, 1060 ft.

Height of Horseshoe Fall, 158 ft.; contour, 3010 ft.

Estimated volume of water passing over both Falls, about 15,000,000 cubic feet per minute, or one cubic mile per week.

Average recession along whole contour Horseshoe Fall, about 2⁴⁄₁₀ ft. per year.

Drop in river from Buffalo to Upper Rapids, 10.36 ft.; from Upper Rapids to brink of Falls, 49 ft.; drop at Falls, 167 ft.; from below Falls to Lower Rapids, 99 ft.; from Lewiston to Lake Ontario, .6 ft.; total fall in River from Lake Erie to Lake Ontario (distance of 37 miles), 326 feet.

Upper Steel Arch Bridge, 1240 ft. long; 47 ft. wide; 190 ft. high; length of arch, 900 ft. Opened to traffic July, 1898.

Lewiston and Queenston Bridge, 840 ft. long; 29 ft. wide; 60 feet high. Opened to traffic July, 1899.

Whirlpool Rapids, current at this point about 27 miles per hour. Depth, 150 to 200 ft.

Whirlpool covers 60 acres, about 200 ft. deep.

Niagara Falls Power Co. (American side). Capacity, 100,000 h.-p.; generating, 100,000 h.-p.

Hydraulic Power Co. of Niagara Falls (American side). Capacity, mechanical h.-p., 150,000; developing mechanical h.-p., 130,000.

Canadian-Niagara Power Co. (Canadian side). Capacity, 75,000 h.-p.; generating, 75,000 h.-p.; under construction, 50,000 h.-p.; total development, when completed, 125,000 h.-p.

Ontario Power Co. (Can. side) Capacity, 160,000 h. p.; generating 160,000 h. p.

5

THE NIAGARA BELT LINE

International Railway—Niagara Gorge Railroad

Toronto Power Co., (Can. side). Generating, 65,000 h.-p.; 87,000 h.-p. under construction; total development, when completed, 152,000 h.-p.

Grand total, when completed, 687,000 h.-p.

Trip around Islands from Prospect Park: van, 20 cts.; automobile, 25 cts.

Maid of the Mist Steamer, including rubber suit, 50 cts.

Cave of the Winds, including rubber suit, $1.00.

Scenic Tunnel (Canadian side), including rubber suit, 50 cts.

NEW YORK STATE RESERVATION

All Niagara Belt Line Cars stop at the main entrance to Prospect Park, where the following points of interest are recommended to visitors:

Gorge View	Cave of the Winds	Prospect Point
Hennipen View	Horseshoe Fall	Green Island
Elevator to View	Three Sister Islands	Goat Island
American Falls	The Spring	Luna Island
from below	Port Day	

Access to all parts of the Reservation is free with the exception of a 5c. charge each way on elevator to view American Falls from below. Visitors are requested to report to the superintendent at the Administration Building, Prospect Park, any violation of the ordinances, extortion or attempt at extortion on the part of the employees, carriage drivers or others upon the Reservation. An official map and guide may be obtained free of charge at any office on the Reservation.

NIAGARA BELT LINE TICKET AGENCIES

Albany, N. Y.........Curtiss, H. J., 426 Broadway.
Brooklyn, N. Y.......D. L. & W. R. R., City Ticket Office, 505 Fulton St.
 Lehigh Valley R. R., City Ticket Office, 30 Flatbush Ave.
Buffalo, N. Y.........International Ry., and all Railroad Ticket Offices.
Boston, Mass.........Beekman Tourist Co., 256 Washington St.
 Marsters Tours, 248 Washington St.
 Raymond & Whitcomb Tourist Co., 306 Washington St.
 Thomas Cook & Son, 336 Washington St.
 Woods, W. H. Tourist Co., 262 Washington St.
Chicago, Ill. ....Grand Trunk Ry., City Ticket Office, 301 So. Clark St.
 Raymond & Whitcomb Tourist Co., 632 So. Michigan Ave.
 Thomas Cook & Son, 15 E. Jackson Boulevard.
 Wabash Railroad, City Ticket Office, 68 West Adams St.
 West Shore, 138 So. Clark St.
Cincinnati, O.........American Tourist Co., 7 E. 4th St.
Cleveland, O.........C. & B. Dock, Ticket Office.
Detroit, Mich.........Det. & Cleveland Nav. Co., Wharf Ticket Office and City Ticket
 Office, 137 Woodward Ave., or Pursers on Steamers.
Jamestown, N. Y.....Chautauqua Traction Co., Excursion Agent.
Lewiston, N. Y.......Niagara Gorge R. R., Ticket Office.
McKeesport, Pa......Carroll, R. G.
Newark, N. J.........D. L. & W. R. R., City Ticket Office, Market and Broad Sts.
 Lehigh Valley R. R., City Ticket Office, 211 Market St.
New York City.......D. L. & W. R. R., Ticket Offices.
 Frank Tourist Co., 398 Broadway.
 Lehigh Valley R. R., City Ticket Office, 94, 401 and 1236 Broadway.
 Marsters Tourist Co., 1246 Broadway.
 McCann Tourist Co., 1328 Broadway.
 Raymond & Whitcomb Tourist Co., 225 Fifth Ave.
 Thomas Cook & Son, 245 and 2389 Broadway, 264 and 553 Fifth Ave.
Niagara Falls, N. Y. Grand Trunk and L. V. R. R., City Ticket Office, Main and Falls Sts.
 International Ry., Terminal Station.
 International Ry., Upper Steel Arch Bridge Ticket Office.
 Niagara Gorge R. R., General Ticket Office, 38 W. Falls St.
Niagara Falls, Ont. International Ry., Upper Steel Arch Bridge Ticket Office.
 Clifton Hotel, Major, G. R.
 International Ry., Bridge St. Station.
Philadelphia, Pa. ... Lehigh Valley R. R., Ticket Office, 900 Chestnut St.
 Phil. & Reading Ry., City Ticket Office, 13th and Chestnut Sts.
 Raymond & Whitcomb Tourist Co., 1005 Chestnut St.
 Thomas Cook & Son, 137 So. Broad St.
Pittsburgh, Pa. ......B. R. & P. Ry., City Ticket Office, Oliver Bldg.
 Raymond & Whitcomb Tourist Co., 86 Vandergrift Bldg.
Quincy, Ill...........Wabash R. R., Ticket Office.
Queenston, Ont......International Ry., Dock Office.
Raleigh, N. C. ....Gattis Tour Co.
Reading, Pa..........Boyer, F. J.
Rochester, N. Y......B. R. & P. Ry., Trav. Pass. Agent, 155 Main St., West.
 Lehigh Valley R. R., City Ticket Office, 67 Main St., East.
St. Catherines, Ont..N. St. C. & T. Ry., Ticket Office.
Springfield, Mass....Raymond & Whitcomb Tourist Co., 389 Main St.
 Wentworth, A. C., 12 East Court St.
Toronto, Ont.........Canada Steamship Lines, City and Wharf Ticket Offices.
Washington, D. C....Balt. & Ohio R. R., City Ticket Office, 1417 "G" St., N. W.
 Beekman Tourist Co., 1416 New York Ave.
Wheeling, W. Va.....W. L. & E. R. R., Ticket Office.

Tickets may be obtained at ticket offices of the New York Central Lines, or from Excursion Agents on New York Central trains and International R'y Yellow Cars entering Niagara Falls, also at principal Ticket Offices Erie R. R.

COPIES OF THIS FOLDER FREE ON APPLICATION

BERT L. JONES, Vice-Pres. and Gen. Mgr.   JOHN EDBAUER, Gen. Passenger Agt.
Niagara Gorge R. R.   Niagara Gorge R. R.
604 Ellicott Square, Buffalo, N. Y.   38 W. Falls St., Niagara Falls, N. Y.
W. J. WHITESIDE, Traffic Agent
International Railway, Main and Court Streets, Buffalo, N. Y.

540M 1-1-16   6

EPILOGUE

The Niagara Falls Power Company, itself owned by the Buffalo, Niagara & Eastern Power Corporation, bought the Niagara Gorge Railroad from I.R.C. on September 1, 1921, in order to gain its important water rights. A short while later, on October 14th, the power company applied for consent to deed the Great Gorge Route to the State in return for the privilege of utilizing water to generate power below the American Falls. It proposed that the State pave a scenic motor highway along the Gorge route. Subsequently the power company attempted to merge the Niagara Gorge Railroad Company into its wholly-owned, freight-only Niagara Junction Railway Company ostensibly to save on operating costs in order to keep the Gorge Route operating. But the Interstate Commerce Commission denied the application on July 19, 1932. I.C.C. accountants had found that the Great Gorge Route was not operating at a loss; it adjusted the company's books to illustrate that the line was making an enormous profit. It turned out that in order to buy the railroad for its water rights, the Niagara Falls Power Company had paid a price greater than the true value of the railroad (placing greater value on the water rights) and had assigned to the railroad company (which it had purchased) the cost of amortizing the $1,949,000 of bonds instead of regarding it as a cost to itself (the borrower). The power company contended that it would have to abandon the Great Gorge Route if the merger were not permitted, but the I.C.C. countered that the parent company could achieve the proposed economies of operation, if it had the will to do so, without merging the companies. I.C.C. examiners concluded, "If abandonment of the railroad properties of the [Niagara] Gorge [Railroad] is threatened, there would seem to be no reason why the power company could not come to the rescue of the [Niagara] Gorge [Railroad] directly instead of through the medium of the [Niagara Junction Railway]." In spite of the exposed book-keeping ruse, the company continued to claim annual losses.

Abandonment and removal of the railway on the Canadian side of the River proved costly to the automobile-oriented Niagara Parks Commission. The reimbursement of International Railway Company for its assets, plus the legal costs of appeals, interest during the period of dispute, interest on the interest to the moment of payment, and the scrapping of the railway (less salvage value of the scrap) amounted to nearly $1,500,000. (The Commission had offered $179,104.) The Privy Council in London settled the disputes over value in 1937 and interest in 1941 (on which the I.R.C. had to pay a Canadian 15% War Tax), and the settlement halted the Parks Commission's ambitious road building program until World War II; the war in turn suspended the plans for many more years. Inasmuch as the Commission was required to pay compensation in terms of replacement value, it would appear in retrospect that a wiser investment would have been for the Commission to bear the costs of relocating the trolley line to accommodate intended landscaping and to contribute toward upgrading of the line and its aging rolling stock. As early as 1952, the Commission was declaring that, "There is

room for more people, but not for automobiles which may be parked."

Often the description of a former electric railway ends with the lament that little evidence remains. However, while much of the Niagara Gorge Belt Line has disappeared, significant remnants can be traced.

The sequence of the following paragraphs follows the course of the Niagara Gorge Belt Line trip.

Vanished Sections:

Falls Street is now a pedestrian mall, itself interrupted by the enclosed Winter Garden occupying the street right-of-way between 1st Street (now Rainbow Boulevard northbound lanes) and Rainbow Boulevard's southbound lanes (parallel to and immediately east of old Main Street). (The center of Main Street, incidentally, remains in the ownership of the New York Central System's successors; this was the original course of the first railroad from Lockport.)

Riverway has disappeared as a street; it now forms the east edge of the Niagara Park Commission's parking lot. The parking lot occupies the site of the International Railway Terminal and carbarns.

A dramatic removal of part of the Belt Line was the January 1938 ice floe that pushed the Honeymoon Bridge off its abutments. The twisted steel structure broke up and floated briefly on the ice, a main portion of it sinking opposite the Niagara Falls sewage disposal plant near the former Falls View carbarn.

Through Victoria Park, most of the railway was replaced by modest landscaping -- essentially lawn -- and the narrow portion was taken into the pavement of the widened Niagara Boulevard.

The present Table Rock House souvenir shop and restaurant is not the original that first was served by the trolleys at its front steps. The newer 1926 facility, which the trolleys served at its rear, is closer to the brink of the Canadian Falls, occupying the site of what was the City of Niagara Falls waterworks pumphouse; the old one was demolished to make way for Niagara Boulevard.

A short distance beyond the newer Table Rock House, the Niagara Parks Commission filled in the raceway of the Park & River Division's power house and converted the building to serve as the Commission's Retail Distribution Center from 1958 to 1982. The Belt Line loop at the Forebay of this plant occupied lawn that is now the People-Mover bus station at the foot of the Horseshoe Falls Incline Railway (which did not exist at the time of the trolleys; it was opened in 1966).

North from Honeymoon Bridge, River Street was widened onto the trolley right-of-way and a stone wall erected along the Gorge edge.

The Sir Adam Beck Generating Station at Queenston Heights was built during 1917-1930 while the trolleys were running, and space for the tracks and road was built into the top of the penstocks. However, when the new Ontario Hydro plant was built during 1950-1958, it obliterated the Gorge wall and trackbeds for the breadth of the plant, although it does provide for the roadway.

The Lewiston-Queenston suspension bridge continued to carry automobile traffic for many years. I.R.C. sold it on July 26, 1939, to Harry P. Schaub for $615,000. On November 1, 1962, the Lewiston-Queenston Arch Bridge opened in conjunction with the Niagara Thruway and the old trolley bridge was removed in 1963.

On the New York side, the construction of the Power Authority of the State of New York (PASNY) power plant obliterated the trackbeds in the Gorge (and did not provide a roadway) for the breadth of the plant. Also, the heavy construction and earth-moving associated with the power plant completely changed the contour of the Gorge and the Niagara Escarpment. The Rome, Watertown & Ogdensburgh (RW&O) line of the New York Central System was used as a truck roadway; its tunnel was dynamited to give adequate clearance. The spoil from the mammoth excavation job was deposited on the escarpment slope (providing the setting for Artpark). PASNY bulldozed the site of historic Fort Gray for the Robert Moses Parkway. Construction of the new Lewiston-Queenston steel arch bridge spilled loose talus onto the Gorge Route trackbeds. South of the PASNY power plant, earth spill from construction of an access roadway to the base of the plant covered a short section of the trackbeds.

In downtown Niagara Falls, the urban renewal program removed 2nd Street from the street network between Niagara Street and Falls Street. The street right-of-way is now occupied by a parking garage.

Discernible Remnants:

The abutments of Honeymoon Bridge can be seen on both sides of the river upstream from the replacement Rainbow Bridge.

While the first (northernmost) of the several bridge spans over the Dufferin Islands was incorporated into the Niagara Boulevard lanes, the second bridge had been changed from steel truss to masonry. The bridge -- its roadway now lawn -- and manicured trackbeds across Dufferin Island remain. The third bridge's abutments now carry a smaller pedestrian bridge.

The Clifton Incline to the *Maid of the Mist* dock remains in place and was used until 1991. The International Railway Company's building, though, had been replaced in 1947 by the present building. In 1977, Von Roll of Switzerland replaced the double-track inclined railway with a higher-capacity single-track line with wider cars that passed on a mid-point siding. Beginning in 1991, prospective boat passengers use a combination stairway and elevator.

After the new Rainbow Bridge was completed just downstream from the Honeymoon Bridge, a spur from the Queen Elizabeth Way was widened to the bridge. Its east-bound roadway occupies the Niagara, St. Catharines & Toronto interurban trackbed. At the underpass of the Michigan Central Railroad, you can notice that the span for this south roadway has a taller clearance -- that was for the interurban's catenary.

Just north of Whirlpool Rapids Bridge, the "Great Gorge Trip" persists in name, at least. The Whirlpool Rapids incline was so renamed when, between 1935 and 1937 it was replaced by an elevator. The walk (not ride) along the foot of the Gorge provides a vantage point from which the trolley roadbed and the Whirlpool Rapids station can be seen on the New York side.

The flat grading for the Whirlpool carbarn remains. The popular Spanish Aerocar still carries worried passengers out to where they can look straight down into the whirlpool. But, they can no longer get off at Thompson's Point. This aerial cableway has been rebuilt several times. Northward from the Spanish Aerocar stop to Bowman Ravine, the double-track trolley roadbed is intact along the Gorge side of the road. When the wheelpit for the Canadian Niagara Powerhouse near the Falls was excavated in 1903, the spoil was used to fill Bowman Ravine, entirely encasing the trolley trestle there, while the line was operating. The tops of the stone abutments, however, can still be seen.

From the trestle all the way to the Sir Adam Beck Generating Station, the double-track trolley roadbed is easily identified by its shaping of the ground which is carefully planted and mowed. Along the way, the former Niagara Glen Inn station building, erected in 1923, continues in service, housing the Niagara Glen Snack Bar and Gift Shop. Automobiles used to park on the vacant trolley trackbeds here, but a parking lot has been provided and the trackbeds landscaped.

The graded trackbeds remain in place from the Sir Adam Beck Generating Station to Queenston Heights Park and down the escarpment to the former Lewiston-Queenston Bridge. After the railway closed, the Queenston Heights Park station was moved to the Niagara Parks Commission's Horticultural School, and the stone entrance gateway to the Sir Isaac Brock monument was moved to its original 1856 location from which it had been transplanted to opposite the trolley station in 1909. The stone towers from which the suspension bridge's cables were slung remain, and on the New York side have been merged into some modern sculpture.

On the Ontario side of the bridge, the former electric railroad to the base of the power plant is today a paved truck road.

On the New York side, the graded trackbeds of both the Great Gorge Route and the RW&O's branch to Lewiston dock can still be found.

In Lewiston, the railroad station area has become a chain super market and parking lot. At the north edge of the lot, the stone portals of the railroad tunnel under Center Street can be seen, although the tunnel has been filled-in.

EPILOGUE

The railway grade through the orchards to Youngstown and Fort Niagara Beach still can be traced.

South from Artpark, the Great Gorge Route trackbeds, were used by construction trucks during building of the PASNY power plant, so remain in place south to the power plant. South of the power plant access road, the double-track trolley roadbed continues, cluttered here and there by rocks and overgrown with trees. It is accessible from a stone stairway down the face of the Gorge at Devil's Hole State Park. As the line progresses southward, it suffers more and more debris from slides of loose talus, generally limiting the flat roadbed to a single-track width and occasionally blocking it entirely, making walking difficult. The trolley stops, observation platforms, and stairways to the water's edge still can be seen.

Since the 1935 rock slide just north of the railroad bridges, additional loose talus has accumulated on a slope that makes walking treacherous. Under the bridges and south of them, the trackbeds are intact, having suffered only a slight amount of erosion. The trackbeds climb the face of the Gorge and pass the Niagara Falls sewage plant, beyond which the trolley line is paved as an access roadway for City trucks.

Following completion of the PASNY power plant project, the New York Central four-track railroad was paved as the Robert Moses Parkway, employing (and somewhat widening) the original railroad bridge over the Great Gorge Route. The now-paved trolley trackway passes under this structure and continues south to Walnut Street where the trolleys once turned onto 2nd Street.

The Schoellkopf power plant collapsed into the Gorge on June 7, 1956, necessitating the hasty construction of the PASNY power project. The top of the plant is occupied by the Schoellkopf Geology Museum; across the Parkway is the Niagara Aquarium.

It is interesting that the Robert Moses Parkway has been found to be offensive and is being systematically removed, grass and trees replacing the twin roadways.

Speculation for the Future:

From the Dufferin Islands to Queenston Heights, visitors to the Canadian side of the Niagara River have a choice of local city buses, double-deck London buses, and the newer bus-type "People-Mover" to travel from attraction to attraction along the rim of the Gorge. But, along the U.S. side, except for the Viewmobile to Goat Island, there is no public transportation. (The tractor-train Viewmobile was initiated by I.R.C.'s successor, the Niagara Frontier Transit System, Inc.)

Several newer generations have no recollection of the fabulous Niagara Gorge Belt Line ride. But, the memory lingers on. From time to time, proposals have been made to restore the Great Gorge Route section of the trip (i.e., the New York side). The possibility was suggested for consideration in the Niagara Frontier Transportation Authority's 1971 Transit Development Program and was revisited during a recent update of that long-range plan. During the 1970s, the City of Niagara Falls entertained proposals from various monorailway and people-mover manufacturers for a downtown shuttle; the prospect of continuing into the Gorge was considered. During 1988-90, the City of Niagara Falls worked with private entrepreneurs on the possibility of running magnetically-levitated cars or a monorailway through downtown, to Canada, and even into the Gorge.

On the Canadian side, consultants for the Niagara Parks Commission in 1988 recommended a vintage trolley line atop the bluff from Marineland, through Falls View, Clifton, and downtown Niagara Falls (Bridge Street) to the Spanish Aerocar at the Whirlpool, with the possibility of continuing to the U.S. over one of the railroad bridges, Rainbow Bridge, or a new low-level bridge well upstream from the Falls. The consultant, Moriyama & Teshima Planners Limited, pointed out that, "Niagara Falls has a tradition of streetcars and the development of a streetcar/pedestrian mall along the ConRail right-of-way interconnecting the tourist activity centres should be explored. Convenience and pedestrian compatibility are more important than speed and high capacity."

Perhaps, the circumstance will come full cycle, and the notion of operating vintage trolleys in Niagara Falls will occur to those agencies that have responsibility for providing transportation improvements.

Steps down from trolley stop to viewing platform, 1974

The Giant Rock, opposite Niagara Glen, May 1982

Its letterboards proclaiming, "Along the Water's Edge for Miles Where No Automobile Can Go!" and "Free and Protected Parking for Autos Provided," car 43's motorman changes poles during The Great Gorge Route's last season.